D0463324

**PRINT CASEBOOKS 8/
THE BEST IN EXHIBITION DESIGN**

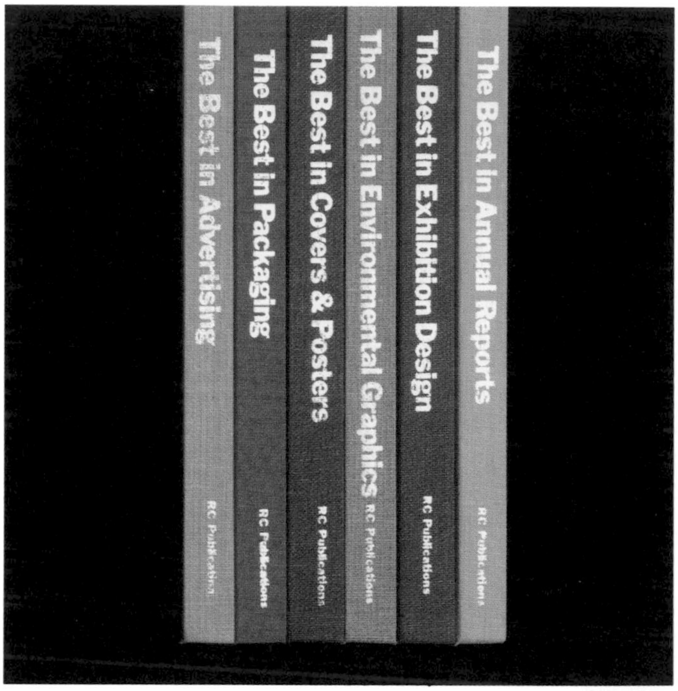
The Best in Advertising
RC Publications
The Best in Packaging
RC Publications
The Best in Covers & Posters
RC Publications
The Best in Environmental Graphics
RC Publications
The Best in Exhibition Design
RC Publications
The Best in Annual Reports
RC Publications

PRINT
CASEBOOKS 8

The Best in Exhibition Design

Written by
Edward K. Carpenter

Published by
**RC Publications, Inc.
Bethesda, MD**

Introduction

Copyright © 1989 by RC Publications, Inc. All rights reserved.

First published 1989 in the United States of America by RC Publications, Inc. 6400 Goldsboro Road Bethesda, MD 20817

No part of this publication may be reproduced or used in any form or by any means—graphic, electronic, or mechanical, including photocopying, recording, taping, or information storage and retrieval systems—without written permission of the publisher.

Manufactured in Hong Kong First Printing 1989

PRINT CASEBOOKS 8/THE BEST IN EXHIBITION DESIGN (1989-90 EDITION)
Library of Congress Catalog Card Number 76-39580
ISBN 0-915734-60-5

PRINT CASEBOOKS 8 (1989-90 EDITION)
Complete 6-Volume Set
ISBN 0-915734-56-7
3-Volume Set No. 1 ISBN 0-915734-63-X
3-Volume Set No. 2 ISBN 0-915734-64-8

RC PUBLICATIONS
President and Publisher: Howard Cadel
Vice President and Editor: Martin Fox
Creative Director: Andrew P. Kner
Managing Editor: Teresa Reese
Art Director: Jim Shefcik
Associate Editor: Tom Goss
Editorial Assistant: Susan Scarfe

As this *Casebook* demonstrates, the backgrounds of people who go into exhibition design are remarkably diverse and wide-ranging. The 25 exhibits seen here are the work of designers who came to exhibits from interior, industrial, and graphic design, as well as from theater design and architecture. Gaillard F. Ravenal, who designed three of these exhibits (at the National Gallery of Art) along with Mark Leithauser and Gordon Anson, has an undergraduate degree in philosophy and a graduate degree in art history. Mark Leithauser trained as an artist and is still a part-time professional artist. Gordon Anson, who does the National Gallery's lighting design and oversees its exhibition production, is one of the new breed of designer with a degree in exhibit design.

Slowly, here and there, exhibition design is beginning to be taught in the schools. Besides Anson, at least two other designers of the exhibits presented here have taken formal courses in exhibit design. Kerry Boyd, exhibit designer at the North Carolina Museum of Art in Raleigh, has a master's degree in exhibition design from California State University in Fullerton, where he was a student of Dextra Frankel's. And Vance Trimble, who designed the Cycle Composites trade exhibit, took Tom Klobe's course in Exhibition Design and Gallery Management at the University of Hawaii. Both Klobe and Frankel have examples of their current work in this *Casebook*, Klobe with two shows at the University of Hawaii Art Gallery, "Polish Posters" and "Art of Micronesia," and Frankel with "Hollywood and History," designed for the Los Angeles County Museum of Art.

Klobe was one of the four jurors who reviewed slides of 186 exhibits in selecting the 25 for inclusion here. Though all juries reflect to an extent the differing personal bents of the jurors, this year's was remarkably like-minded. If jurors showed a collective prejudice, it was against cliché. For example, the time-line, the graphic display used so often to explain an exhibit's content historically, is noticeably lacking from the selections they made. In general, it seems that exhibit time-lines are being replaced by audiovisual shows tucked in a niche or a separate room at an exhibit's beginning or sometimes at the end. If these slide programs themselves are becoming a cliché, it may not matter. For one thing, they are positioned outside the traditional exhibit fabric. Then, too, an exhibit must have something to help visitors orient themselves within it. To eschew an effective way of doing this merely to avoid sameness might be flouting reason.

By using slide programs and films, often running on continuous loops at several places within an exhibit, designers are able to do away with panels of text that in the past have competed for space with artifacts and art. Indeed, the exhibits seen here show an increasing turn toward an orderly, uncluttered look, and it may be that using video monitors and slide shows to convey information is more responsible for this look than any bias of the jurors. Whatever the reason, in none of these exhibits is a visitor put off by a seemingly overwhelming amount of art, artifact or text.

In general, the amount of text in exhibits is being reduced, and sometimes whatever text there is is being presented not just to be read but to be *inviting* to read. Tom Geismar of MetaForm, which designed the Statue of Liberty exhibit, says he found that keeping blocks of text brief, and making the type large, lured more visitors into stopping to read. Chester Design Associates, who designed "In Bondage and Freedom" for Richmond's Valentine Museum, found, through a formal evaluation, that visitors were ignoring text and headings placed overhead and reading only some of the text at eye-level or below.

Another concern of the jury was exhibit frameworks or backgrounds. If, in their opinion, the background overshadowed whatever was being displayed, the jurors rejected the exhibit. They felt the ideal exhibit was one in which (among other things) the exhibit design enhanced and clarified whatever was being exhibited, without upstaging it. Their concern was not that an exhibit background be minimal, but that it be appropriate. Indeed, at least two of the winning exhibits had quite elaborate frameworks. In their design for "Treasure Houses of Britain," the National Gallery of Art's exhibit design staff created appropriate settings for paintings, furniture, sculpture

and other artifacts from British country houses by setting up rooms for them that combined details from rooms in these houses. For "Chicago Architecture," Stanley Tigerman designed an architectural framework that, while elaborate, enhanced the drawings, plans and models it surrounded.

In at least one instance, the exhibit framework was the only criterion the jury had for deciding whether to include the exhibit in this *Casebook*. The exhibit within the framework consisted entirely of information controlled by a computer which visitors could call forth on touch-sensitive video screens. One or two terminals in "Promise of Permanency" could display as much as two hours of information stored on laser disks. Designed, like the information on the disks, by Albert Woods Design for the National Park Service, the exhibit's framework was eye-catching enough to lure visitors, while its design conveyed enough care and excitement to appeal to the jurors. Woods used his framework to bring in visitors the way the bright lights of the old-time movie marquees attracted moviegoers. Seen from afar, his framework offered the promise of something important and exciting, but he also meant it to provide a constant reminder of the exhibit theme—the promise and permanency of the U.S. Constitution.

It seems to this observer, who sat alongside the jurors as they reviewed the entries, that the level of exhibit design is high but that exhibit designers are still at the same plateau of

achievement that they attained some years ago. No hummocks of innovation are in evidence—certainly nothing that promises to change the way the public perceives exhibitions and the way designers approach them. Computer-linked, touch-activated video screens give exhibits the capability of offering an unusual depth of information, and could change the way exhibits are designed. But these screens and the computers that link them are still expensive. Moreover, they require considerable technical expertise to program and set up and are (for these reasons) not yet widely used.

It would seem that innovation might come through research. Determining just how people visit an exhibit, finding out how they move through it, what they read or don't read, whether or not they enjoy using touch screens or reading text in captions and labels would give exhibit designers guidelines for design. Where should text be put and how should it be presented so people will read it? Now and then, such research is done, but rarely do the results reach a wide audience in readily digestible form. Almost anything that would tell exhibit designers how better to reach their audience could lead to improved exhibit design. And the cost of the evaluation can be budgeted with the funding. Money for the Valentine Museum's evaluation of "In Bondage and Freedom" came wrapped in funding for the entire exhibit from the National Endowment for the Humanities.

Money for the other exhibits and their design came from many sources, often from the

combined pockets of private individuals, government agencies, and corporations. Many corporations have come to realize that exhibits at trade shows must be well-designed to be competitive, and that corporate exhibits of almost any type are an effective way of presenting a corporate message. For some time, corporations have realized, too, that exhibits are a way to project an image of patronage and cooperation. Thus, the Ford Motor Company was willing to put up over a million dollars to ensure an exhibit of the scope and excitement of "Treasure Houses of Britain." Those who want to mount an exhibition, therefore, turn to corporations as well as to the government and wealthy individuals for the money they need. Philip Caldwell, chairman of the Ford Motor Company, for one, questions this quick reflex. He has been quoted as saying: "Encouragement of the arts should not depend primarily on either the patronage of a few modern Medicis or government grants. Instead, business enterprises and individuals at every level should, within their capabilities, assist with the funding, facilities, personnel and active support for the arts, not only in their own self-interest but also for the support of the large human community to which we all belong." This wider support Caldwell talks of is occasionally evident. Needing more than a million dollars to build a habitat for some Nepalese snow leopards, the Bronx Zoo turned over fund-raising to the Zoo's Women's Auxiliary, which came back with the money.

Cost of the 25 exhibits in this *Casebook* ranged from the $4 million the National Park Service spent on the Statue of Liberty exhibit (the money was raised from public donations as part of the statue's restoration for its 100th birthday) to the $2000 the University of Hawaii Art Gallery spent for an exhibition of Polish posters. Five of these exhibits cost more than a million dollars.

Of the exhibits seen here, the majority (14) appeared in museums. Seven of these were art exhibits. Two were costume shows. One was an architecture exhibit, and one a permanent exhibit for a science museum. Four of the winners were trade shows and three were corporate exhibits. Two were designed for the National Park Service and two were zoo exhibits.

That exhibits reflect what has the world's attention is again abundantly clear. The U.S. is curious about Japan and the Japanese are eager to have us understand them. The result is a slew of exhibits about Japan in a wonderful array of guises. Two of these are seen here: one an exhibit of kimonos at the North Carolina Museum of Art and the other a show of commissioned art and ancient artifacts at the Walker Art Gallery in Minneapolis.

This *Casebook* offers something of interest for most exhibit designers, except possibly those who would like to see a review of World's-Fair design, which has supplied *Casebook* winners in the past. This edition, no World's Fairs.

However, the New York Zoological Society's Bronx Zoo is on a scale matching some World's Fairs. The zoo is leading the way in designing environments that benefit both the animals that live in them and the visitors who view them. This *Casebook* features the Bronx Zoo's Himalayan Highlands which simulates a few acres of Nepal for millions of visitors who are unlikely to see either Nepal or the Himalaya. Displays such as these are important if city dwellers are going to understand natural environments; they give the zoo a chance to explain why these environments are important for all of us.

In designing exhibits and a graphic program for another famous zoo—Lincoln Park Zoo in Chicago—the Memphis design firm of Bedno/Bedno showed the zoo administrators that good design can draw people in and keep them there and maybe even cause them to leave a little better informed. Bedno/Bedno's work probably left the administration there more conscious of good design than it had been, and helped the zoo to compete more successfully with Chicago's other attractions for attendance.

Carter Brown, head of the National Gallery of Art, is, among other things, part designer. There is no question that during his administration exhibit design has flourished at the National Gallery. Brown is living proof that design-conscious executives create design-conscious institutions. And a review of the winning exhibitions in this *Casebook* points up the fact that one of the exhibit designer's many jobs is to create this consciousness.
—*Edward K. Carpenter*

Casebook Writer

Edward K. Carpenter

For many years an editor with national architectural and design magazines, Edward K. Carpenter writes extensively in both fields. He is the author of books on urban design, environmental design and industrial design as well as exhibition design. This is his seventh *Exhibition Design Casebook*.

Tom Klobe

In 1977, Tom Klobe became director of the University of Hawaii Art Gallery. Since then, with Klobe designing the gallery's exhibits, raising money to fund them and supervising their installations, the gallery has gained an international reputation for the quality of its exhibits. Grants to support the exhibits have come from private foundations and corporations and from the National Endowment for the Arts (11), the State Foundation on Culture and the Arts (15), and the Hawaii Committee for the Humanities (4). Seven traveling exhibits organized by the UH Art Gallery have traveled to 68 museums in the U.S., Mexico, Canada, Japan and Taiwan.

Klobe, who has a bachelor's and a master's degree in design from the University of Hawaii and who spent a year studying toward a doctorate in art history at UCLA, teaches courses at the University of Hawaii in exhibition design and gallery management, in beginning and intermediate design and in Islamic and Medieval art history. His exhibits have been seen in previous *Exhibition Design Casebooks*.

Elizabeth Miles

Elizabeth Miles is a principal and senior exhibit designer with Miles Fridberg Molinaroli, Inc., a firm she founded in 1983 with David Fridberg and Richard Molinaroli. Located in Washington, DC, the firm designs exhibits and graphics for museums, institutions and commercial clients. Miles has a BFA in graphic design from Rhode Island School of Design and did independent study in graphic design at the Allgemeine Gewerbeschule in Basil, Switzerland. For almost ten years she worked in exhibition design at the Smithsonian's National Museum of Natural History, becoming chief exhibition designer there. Her recent exhibitions include "Tropical Rainforests: A Disappearing Treasure," done for the Smithsonian Institution's Traveling Exhibition Service; "That Exceptional One: Women in American Architecture, 1888-1988," designed for the American Institute of Architects; and "Closing in on Cancer for the National Institutes of Health." Two exhibits designed by Miles were honored in previous *Exhibition Design Casebooks*.

Gaillard F. Ravenel

As a Kress Fellow at the National Gallery of Art in 1969, Gaillard F. Ravenel hung a Durer show—"Dürer in America: His Graphic Work." Following that, Ravenel stayed on at the National Gallery and since 1973, when the Gallery set up a Department of Design and Installation, Ravenel has been its chief. He points out, however, that despite his title, all the Gallery's exhibition design is a co-equal collaboration among himself and his departmental colleagues, Mark Leithauser and Gordon Anson. Ravenel has degrees in philosophy (Duke University) and an M.A. in art history from the University of North Carolina, and in addition to being the designer, his involvement in the National Gallery's exhibitions has often been, at least in part, as a curator. A number of the National Gallery's exhibitions that Ravenel helped design have been winners in previous *Exhibition Design Casebooks*.

Bruce Burdick

With his design partner and wife Susan Kosakowsky Burdick, Bruce Burdick operates The Burdick Group in San Francisco. They work on a broad range of design projects including, among other things, furniture, exhibit systems, and retail space, as well as exhibitions. Burdick majored in architecture and industrial design at the University of Southern California and Art Center College, and from 1971 to 1974 he directed the Department of Environmental Design at the Art Center. Before opening his own office in 1970, he worked as a designer for Charles Eames, John Follis and Herb Rosenthal. In 1974, The Burdick Group moved to San Francisco.

The Burdick Group's work was included in Time magazine's "Ten Best Designs of 1982" and the firm has been recipient of the Industrial Designers Society of America's Award of Honor. Several Burdick designs appeared in previous *Exhibition Design Casebooks*.

Design Firms/Designers
Consultants/Curators

A Promise of Permanency:
The U.S. Constitution through 200 Years

1.

In Philadelphia's Independence National Historical Park, across from Independence Hall, is a glass building left from the nation's Bicentennial celebration in 1976. From 1976 to 1987, it was a sort of general information kiosk, its 4500 sq. ft. filled sporadically with a series of temporary exhibits. Then, for the celebration of the 200th anniversary of the U.S. Constitution, the National Park Service decided it wanted an exhibit that used contemporary electronic media to convey the way the Constitution has been, and continues to be, an integral part of the way we live. Another exhibit, in a nearby bank building, would use more conventional exhibit techniques of artifacts and documents to tell the Constitution's story up to its ratification. The Park Service wanted the electronic media exhibit to explain how the Constitution works and why it has held up for so long, and how it has provided a framework for the great changes that have taken place in the U.S. since the Constitution was ratified 200 years ago. And they

wanted it done without artifacts.

Albert Woods Design Associates, who prepared the exhibit on a $1,000,000 budget, used computers linked to video screens which visitors touched to call forth specific messages from video disks. Says Albert Woods, "The exhibit thus became more like a stage set for the interactive media. The challenge was to integrate these media into an exhibit landscape." The challenge was also to gather film clips and other visual images that would tell the story of the Constitution, its amendments, and the court cases that have refined and shaped it to handle the changes of a growing, evolving society of 240 million individuals.

The landscape devised by the Albert Woods designers had three distinct sections. First, there was a serpentine wall framed with metal studs and covered with two thicknesses of ½" sheet rock that snaked for some 180' around two sides of the space. Behind the wall, they left a corridor wide enough for

2.

3.

4.

personnel to use when servicing the audiovisual equipment. In the wall, they recessed five alcoves for video monitors, each alcove carpeted with a dark-ribbed carpet to help absorb sound and light. On the serpentine wall, they pasted a wallpaper collage that had been mocked up, then photographed, of some of the most familiar images from our country's history. The tops of these images, rising 30' above the floor, are cut out, so that—for example—the heads of Chief Justice John Marshall, Civil War soldiers, slaves, Conestoga wagons, the Wright Brothers plane, the cloud rising from an atom bomb blast and the flag being raised by the Marines at Iwo Jima, all appear silhouetted by the light from the windows behind them. Lincoln, Martin Luther King, an astronaut walking on the moon, a poster with Uncle Sam saying "I Want You," a photo of a sailor kissing a nurse in Times Square on V-J Day, the golden spike being driven in to complete the transcontinental railway, are among the many other images

1. Photo-collage wall of scenes from American history undulates 180' around two sides of the exhibit space, forming a backdrop.
2-5. Core of exhibit is on touch-sensitive video terminals. Visitors touch screens to call up information on the U.S. Constitution.
6. Video viewing alcoves are built into the perimeter wall.

1.

that form the backdrop against which Woods and his designers positioned the video terminals that told about the Constitution. Except for a blue carpet on the floor, Woods kept the elements throughout the space black-and-white and gray so that the color images on the video monitors would stand out.

Within the space defined by the undulating photo-collage wall, the complete text of the Constitution and its amendments is displayed on a 10'-high, semicircular wall made of Avonite, a hard plastic that resembles polished granite or marble. Cupped by this semicircular wall are a group of five video consoles on floor stands that run a program (evoked by a touch on the screens) telling how the Constitution works. It would take two hours to run through all of the computer's information on that program.

In the undulating outer wall, each of the five alcoves contains three video screens, a 13″ screen at chest level and two 19″ screens in the wall at the top of the alcove, which can be

6.

seen by a group standing nearby. Visitors can call up a program (composed of archival film, graphics, text and photos) on how the Constitution has weathered political, cultural and economic change since its ratification in 1787. This program can keep anyone who has the stamina and interest occupied for 2½ hours.

Also in the exhibit space are a grouping of nine 10'-high, 6'-wide towers. Inset in each of these are two video screens—again, a 13″ screen is placed at chest level, and one measuring 19″ is placed higher so it can be seen by several viewers. Each video here covers a single topic, such as the death penalty, sex discrimination, freedom of speech, etc. Each four-minute loop consists of an opening statement followed by two opposing statements. At the end, viewers are asked to touch the video screen to register their feelings about the issue. On the inner side of each tower around the video screens is a photo blowup illustrating the issue. The death-penalty tower, for instance, has a black-and-

white mural of a death-row prisoner peering out from behind bars.

One of the initial problems faced by designer Albert Woods was the projection of ventilation shafts up through the floor into the space. Instead of working them into the exhibit or working around them, he covered the protruding shafts with a platform curved gracefully on two sides, and on this platform he set the exhibit. Beneath it ran the cables and electrical connections needed to connect video screens and computers and to supply them power.

Another intrusion is the original space was an air fountain. It rises about 30′ high next to a ramp that leads up onto the platform. Woods sheathed the tower in laminate and Avonite and made it into a title tower with "200" in red neon at the top and an Avonite plaque that gives the show title, "Promise of Permanency." Inside, along with the air ducts, is space for racks that hold the computers and video disk equipment.

Woods gave the exhibit space one splash of color, besides the images on the video terminals. Over the central part of the exhibit, where the Constitution is printed on the semicircular wall, he placed a dozen or so of the red, white, and blue half-circle banners with red centers and a periphery of white stars in a blue field that you see at political conventions or on 4th of July speakers' platforms.

For typefaces, Woods selected Frutiger and Garamond Stempel for what he considers their classic, traditional, monumental quality" and because they are easy to read.

7.

8.

9.

10.

11.

The Albert Woods designers put the exhibit together, designing the interactive computer video hook-up programs (working with IBM, which donated the equipment), selecting all photographs and film footage and arranging for rights, preparing models and working drawings and supervising construction, all in one year.

"Promise of Permanency" is taken from what Benjamin Franklin wrote in 1789, that "our new Constitution is now established, and has an appearance that promises permanency . . ."

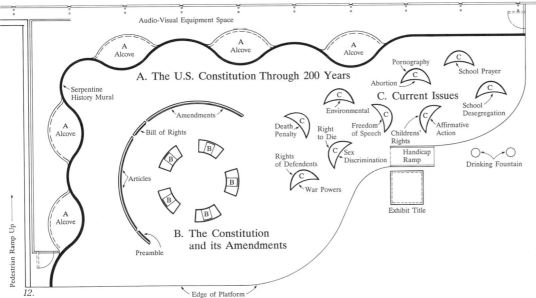

Audio-Visual Equipment Space

A Alcove   A Alcove   A Alcove

A. The U.S. Constitution Through 200 Years

Serpentine History Mural

A Alcove

Amendments

Bill of Rights

Articles

A Alcove

Preamble

B. The Constitution and its Amendments

Pornography   C School Prayer

Abortion   C

C. Current Issues

Environmental   C

Death Penalty   C   Right to Die   Freedom of Speech   C   School Desegregation   C

Rights of Defendents   C Sex Discrimination   Childrens' Rights   Affirmative Action

Handicap Ramp   Drinking Fountain

War Powers

Exhibit Title

Pedestrian Ramp Up

12.

Edge of Platform

Client: U.S. National Park Service, Dept. of the Interior (Philadelphia)
Sponsor: Bell of Pennsylvania, a Bell Atlantic Co.
Design firm: Albert Woods Design Associates, Inc., New York City
Designers: Albert Woods (project director and chief designer); Masahiro Ogyu, George S. Kanelba, Lorelei Guttman (exhibition design); Fred Karp, Louis Cutrona, Tom Nicholson, Torben Schioler, Colin Cook, Jane Abbott (interactive program production); Ileana Truneanu, Peter Galperin, May Liu, Greg Mastrianno, Bettina Bottome, Patrick McCabe (graphic design); Hank Whittemore (script); Herman Eberhardt (research director); Heather Cook, Katharine McKenna (research and coordination); Esther Brumberg, Anne Hobart, George Hobart, Carousel Research, Inc., Linda Christensen, Rosemary Eakins (photographic research)
Consultants: Dr. G. Alan Tarr, Dr. Jeffrey Morris, Dr. Eugene Hickok, Jr. (subject matter); Donald Bliss (lighting)
Fabrication: Charles M. Maltbie Associates

7, 8. Cupped by a 10'-high semi-circular wall on which the Constitution is printed, five video monitors tell how the Constitution works.
9. Thirty-foot-high air tower becomes a showcase for exhibit title. Inside tower is space for computer and video equipment.
10, 11. Each of nine towers with inset video screens covers a topic, such as freedom of speech, affected by the Constitution.
12. Floor plan.

13/Exhibition Design

The Statue of Liberty

When the Statue of Liberty was repaired and refurbished for her 100th birthday, part of the money raised for the project went toward a permanent exhibit in the statue's base. Designed by MetaForm, Inc., the exhibit is, according to a panel at the exhibit entrance, "her biography." It is also, the panel goes on to say, "a tribute to the people who created her, to those who built and paid for her, to the ideals she represents and to the hopes she inspires."

MetaForm is a corporation formed by the design firm of Chermayeff & Geismar in New York City when Jack Masey left the State Department in 1979 to become a partner. Masey is in charge of MetaForm, which takes on certain, usually complex, exhibition projects, often for the government. Client for the Statue of Liberty exhibit was the National Park Service.

The MetaForm designers had an awkward space to work with. Originally intended for offices in the statue's base, the space is essentially a U-shaped corridor averaging about 8½' high and 22' wide. In all, there are some 7500 sq. ft. and within that the designers had to accommodate a lot of utility ducts and lighting. Most of the lights ended up fitting into the tops of the display cases, which snake along the space's outer wall.

MetaForm divided the exhibit into two sections, which flow smoothly into one another, one dealing with the statue's history, the other with its symbolism. But actually, the exhibit starts in the base's central lobby, where the statue's old torch, which had badly deteriorated and was replaced, is now set up. On the mezzanine overlooking the torch are backlighted, table-mounted panels of text and graphics, raised 23″ off the floor. These explain how the torch came to be modified with glass panes and interior lighting and how leaks where glass met frame caused deterioration. The new torch is solid again, as the statue's French sculptor, Auguste Bartholdi, originally intended. And it is lighted from the outside.

2.

Farther along the mezzanine, you enter the exhibit through bronze doors and almost immediately confront Miss Liberty's full-sized head. It is an exact replica and could, in the event that the real statue head is damaged, be substituted for it. The exhibit designers had the replica made in France along with a duplicate of the statue's left foot (which appears later in the exhibit) because they wanted visitors to be able to walk up and touch and be photographed with them. The head alone is bigger than an entire human: 8' tall. Her nose is 4½' long; her mouth, 3' wide; her eyes, 2½' across.

1. Sketch of portion of exhibit space. At right is full-scale replica of Miss Liberty's left foot.
2. Display case with Liberty statuettes.
3. Full-sized replica of Miss Liberty's head. Nose is 4½' long.

3.

1.

Just beyond the head, the wall cases start, and in these the designers piece together the story of how the statue came to be and made its way to New York harbor. Through a delightful composition of sculptures, photomurals, photographs, etchings, and text—one which is never crowded or hurried—visitors learn how two Frenchmen, historian Edouard de Laboulaye and Bartholdi carried out Laboulaye's idea of a gift from France to the U.S. The case along the first 120′ wing of the exhibit's U-shaped space is open. There is no protective (and glare-producing) barrier of plexiglass. Anything fragile that cannot be anchored securely, such as small models of the statue, is in a vitrine. A caption bar about a foot wide positioned 23″ off the floor, so it can be read by children or those in wheelchairs, keeps visitors back from the case interior. Besides captions on the caption bar, the designers have occasional blocks of text screened on the walls beneath a blue label band at the top of the case's back wall. All type is Century Old Style bold in sizes from ½″ to 5″ cap height. Century Old Style was designed around the time the statue was created and, says Tom Geismar, who was one of the exhibit's designers, "it's available and easy to read." The designers tried to limit the amount of text, presenting it in what Geismar calls "understandable bites." And by printing it in large type, they helped to make it inviting to read. The same concept seems to have guided the entire exhibit design.

The items assembled for display are impressive, evocative and fun. Besides the full-sized Liberty head and foot, there is a plaster model of the statue's left ear from Bartholdi's studio. A workshop was set up with casts, molds and tools used to create the statue's copper skin (by the repoussé method). A series of maquette replicas traces the statue's design development. The designers rescued the original plaque with its Emma Lazarus poem ("Give me your tired, your poor, Your huddled masses . . ."). It had been taken off the statue's base and put in storage 70 or 80 years ago. They commissioned, and set up in the central part of the space, an 8′ cut-away model (from a casting of a model by Bartholdi) showing the internal support structure designed by Gustav Eiffel (who would eventually build a tower in Paris) to hold the statue up in New York Harbor's heat, cold and possible gale-force winds.

MetaForm put together four video loops—one making the extra Miss Liberty foot, one showing a computer-generated structural analysis of the statue, one a pastiche of print advertisements for the statue, and one of the dedication ceremony and parades when the statue originally opened. These films play on monitors set at eye level on the wall opposite the display cases.

Three scale models of architect Richard Morris Hunt's design concepts for the statue's pedestal were commissioned by MetaForm to help tell the story of how the U.S. raised $300,000 to have the pedestal built.

4.

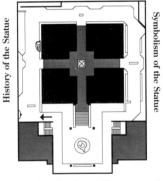

History of the Statue

History of the Statue

Symbolism of the Statue

The Torch and Flame   5.

4. *Model of Ellis Island renovation.*
5. *Floor plan.*
6. *World War I Liberty Loan posters in wall case.*
7. *Miss Liberty's old torch, replaced in renovation project, stands at exhibit entrance.*

The exhibit's second section tells how the statue has become a symbol of freedom. A good deal of the work MetaForm did for the exhibit was in ferreting out items for display and in this second section they outdid themselves. Probably one of the section's two most impressive displays is an 8'-by-10' mirrored case holding four shelves of Liberty statuettes. The other is a free-standing wall, 8'-by-10', each side of which is covered with a mosaic image of the statue made of picture postcards bearing her image.

In this section, the wall case is enclosed with Herculite glass doors, sealed with silicone. And in the cases are hoards of items that show how the statue's image has been used to sell and inspire. Rummaging through antique stores, talking to collectors and poring over letters written to the Statue of Liberty-Ellis Island Foundation, which raised money for the restoration (and the exhibit), the designers found the hundreds of items they display. There are travel posters, Liberty Bond posters, sheet-music covers, pieces of folk art (such as the white quilt with the picture of the Statue of Liberty in the middle), medals and programs from the 1886 dedication parade. All these the designers mounted and hung, filling the wall case space three-dimensionally. And even here, by their arrangement of shapes, colors and sizes, they have avoided a sense of clutter. Red text panels with white lettering stand out clearly against the welter of color around them.

In one space, the designers

6.

7.

mounted letters from immigrants telling how they felt when they first sighted the Statue of Liberty. These were mounted in a plexiglass sandwich slanted at 45 degrees, and screened on above them were hanging plexiglass panel blowups of segments of the letters. All of these have as a backdrop a photo blowup of the Statue of Liberty and Ellis Island seen from the deck of a ship, its rails lined with people. One of the letter fragments reads, "A boy was screaming with joy, 'Wake up, wake up, you can see the Statue of Liberty—you can see the Statue of Liberty.' "

The exhibit ends as it began, with an image of the statue. At the end of the final corridor of the U-shaped exhibit space is a 7'-by-9'-by-10' rear-lighted transparency of the restored statue holding up her shining torch.

MetaForm undertook the exhibit design under the blanket of a group formed for the purpose. The Park Service wanted to turn the entire job over to a group which could complete it from conception to installation and to that end MetaForm collaborated with Rathe Productions, Inc., New York City, and with Design and Production, Inc., Alexandria, Virginia. They called themselves The Liberty/Ellis Island Collaborative.

The work was completed on a budget of $4 million, which included money for exterior wayside exhibits on Ellis Island and signs. And the design, finding everything and putting it all in place, took about one and a half years.

8.

9.

10.

Client: U.S. Dept. of Interior, National Park Service; Gary Roth, project manager
Funding agency: Statue of Liberty-Ellis Island Foundation
Design firm: MetaForm, Inc., New York City
Designers: Jack Masey (project manager), Ivan Chermayeff (principal), Thomas Geismar (principal designer), John P. Grady (principal designer), Stephan Geissbuhler (principal), Phyllis Montgomery (director of research), Christina Trimble (project coordinator), Louis Scrima, Gary Stilovich (senior designers), Gail C. Boyajian, Eileen Dolan, Chris Farley, Karen Gibbons, Jim Gratson, Hyun Joo Kim, Robert Henry, Michelle Meade, Neal Spitzer, Sue Willis (design staff), Mary-Angela E. Hardwick (senior researcher)
Fabricators Rathe Productions, Inc.; Design and Production, Inc.

8. Rear-lighted transparency of statue at exhibit's end.
9. Photo blowup of Auguste Bartholdi's Parisian workshop at work on the statue.
10. Examples of use of the statue's image.

Magnificent Voyagers:
The U.S. Exploring Expedition, 1838-1842

In 1838, when the U.S. was still a relatively young nation, it sent out its first globe-circling scientific expedition. Under the leadership of Navy Lt. Charles Wilkes, the expedition made a treaty in the Philippines with groups that had been harassing our shipping, charted much of the Pacific, and established for the first time that Antarctica is a continent by sailing 1500 miles along its shore. (For years, the French disputed our claim saying they'd been first to make the discovery.) Besides charts, the expedition brought back in its six ships collections of plants and animals and of artifacts used by peoples around the world. If there wasn't enough stuff to sink a ship, there was at least enough, when added to collections already on hand in Washington, to make the government realize it had a storage problem, and out of that realization grew the Smithsonian Institution.

The exhibit that Richard Molinaroli of Miles Fridberg Molinaroli designed for the Smithsonian some 143 years after the U.S. Exploring Expedition returned home was meant in part to celebrate the 75th anniversary of the opening of the Smithsonian's National Museum of Natural History, which houses the artifacts Wilkes and his ships collected. None of these artifacts had been displayed since the middle of the 19th century. Though they had been on view a few years after the expedition first came home, in the building that is now the National Portrait Gallery, they had been in storage for well over a century before Molinaroli went to work and put together the exhibit

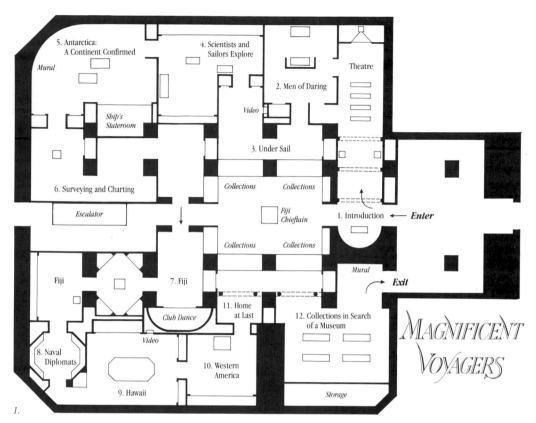

1.

1. *Floor plan.*
2. *Early perspective rendering of how the exhibit entrance might be designed. Note that exhibit title changed.*

2.

that ran at the NMNH for a year.

Actually, for two years before Molinaroli was asked in, Jane Walsh of the Smithsonian's Department of Anthropology had been digging out and assembling the Wilkes expedition artifacts. Buried here and there in storage areas throughout the NMNH, the expedition's artifacts had been neglected the way things in attics often are. Some had deteriorated beyond hope of repair. And they were stored in no particular order. In fact, Walsh had to go through the museum with notes and diaries made by expedition members in which they had noted what was collected, trying to match items in storage to those mentioned.

Once she had assembled these in one area, Molinaroli spent what he estimates was about 50 per cent of his time for nine months going over the items and helping select what might best be displayed in the exhibit. In all, they chose some 1700 items. After that, Molinaroli went to work in earnest, spending most of his time for the next year designing the exhibit and seeing it put in place.

In all, it was given 13,000 sq. ft. of space in the museum's Evans Gallery. The space was awkward. For one thing, a corridor cut the gallery in half and people were constantly walking through this corridor on their way elsewhere. The gallery also had as many as 21 supporting columns. Molinaroli worked both the columns and the corridor into his design for the space, building wall cases around the columns and tearing out walls to tie at least part of

3.

4.

5.

3. Western America section with artifacts collected by the Expedition.
4. Dancing Fijian figure in wall case before an enlarged reproduction of an engraving which shows Fijians dancing for the Exploring Expedition.
5. Naval Diplomats section with artifacts recounting treaty made by Expedition in the Philippines. Expedition engravings were reproduced directly on walls.

6.

7.

the corridor into the gallery. Important time was also spent organizing the exhibit so that it told the story of the Exploring Expedition of 1838-1842 coherently and understandably. The plan involved 13 thematic sections, which Molinaroli set up in 18 rooms. The sections were: Introduction (including a small theater), Men of Daring, Under Sail, Scientists and Sailors Explore, Antarctica–A Continent Confirmed, Surveying and Charting, Fiji, Naval Diplomats, Hawaii, Western America, Home at Last, Collections in Search of a Museum, and the Collections of the Exploring Expedition.

Molinaroli positioned the last of these sections in the corridor between the gallery's two halves, opening up the walls and replacing them with 9′-high double-sided glass cases. These cases not only held 1000 objects from the expedition, but let visitors see through on both sides into the rest of the exhibit, which wrapped around this central space. One entered the gallery through a portal topped by the show title, "Magnificent Voyagers," in type that spoke of daring and romance, a special face designed by one of Molinaroli's partners, David Fridberg.

Through the entrance, one saw past an introductory area to a 9′-high glass case in the center of the Collections area, which held, on a platform covered with brown silk, a life-sized mannikin of a Fijian chieftain wrapped in 300 feet of tapa cloth (cloth made from the inner bark of mulberry trees). The expedition had brought back the cloth, and the museum arranged it on the mannikin as it

6. *See-through cases with biological specimens collected by the Expedition.*
7. *Wall case with layers of Polynesian artifacts.*
8. *Mural in Antarctic section was 54′ long.*

8.

appeared to be worn by Fijian chieftains in old engravings. The museum made the mannikin, too, using as model a Fijian from the Fiji embassy in Washington, a tall, well-built man with a mustache, recreating his face without the mustache. Set in the glass case, the tapa-wrapped figure drew people into the exhibit.

The introductory area told a story without words. On a curved, 12′-broad wall, Molinaroli placed an 8′-high blowup of expedition leader Wilkes's orginal world chart, redrawn on photo paper and mounted on ¼″ Masonite over poplar framing. On this chart were the routes followed by the expedition's six ships in their four-year odyssey. A few feet in front of the chart, Molinaroli positioned a model of Wilkes's flagship, *Vincennes*. Made some years after the expedition, this model, 4½′ from stem to stern, was resurrected for the exhibit. Molinaroli mounted it on a sheet of clear plexiglass, the ship riding the top edge of the plexi on metal clamps, and set in a floor-to-ceiling clear plexiglass case with a light box at its top. If you looked through the case to the wall chart, the ship seemed to be riding the seas of the chart.

To offer more explanation of the expedition's goals and accomplishments and how it led to the birth of the Smithsonian, a film, suggested by Molinaroli and made by the museum, was set up at the end of a corridor-like space to the right of the entrance. You approached a small theater with fixed benches through an area of beams and trusses, planked walls and

overhead gratings, as if going aboard a ship.

Throughout the exhibit, Molinaroli achieved a 19th-century mood through his choice of colors and detailing. For instance, he cut doorways between rooms in silhouettes of 19th-century arches, and moldings on cases and ceiling edges were cut and polished in 19th-century patterns. For colors, he used rich, usually deep colors, often blues or indigos evocative of the sea. There were two rooms with a long common wall covered floor to ceiling by charts and maps in rich mahogany frames. There were instruments and engravings and documents and letters in cases and frames. At one critical point, where the exhibit flow had to cross the central corridor, Molinaroli lessened the intrusion by setting up (at right angles to the door leading to the corridor) a wall case filled with brass scientific instruments through which you could see to the central collections area with the figure of the Fijian chief in his tapa wraps. Straight ahead, through the doorway in the exhibit room across the corridor, you saw a full-sized dancing Fijian in front of a diorama made from a photomural enlargement of an engraving in the official Wilkes report. The dance was the ceremonial "club dance," performed for the expedition by the Fijians. Music from the dance, recorded at various times over the years, played in the background.

For the Antarctic room, Molinaroli commissioned a 54′-long-by-12′-high mural showing

9.

10.

a Wilkes ship sighting a French ship on the Antarctic coast in January 1840. At Molinaroli's suggestion, artist Hugh McKay gave the mural a slightly fantastic feeling, setting it apart from 20th-century realism in an effort to create a 19th-century mood.

Probably the exhibit's most fragile item was a 15'-long, 7' wide piece of highly-decorated tapa cloth. Molinaroli mounted it in an 11'-high wall case on a sloped platform to give it full support, holding it in place at the top with a plexiglass strip. Beneath the case, behind a 10"-high baseboard, were trays of silica gel to hold down the moisture around the tapa.

Molinaroli silk-screened a considerable amount of text and labels right on the walls or risers within the cases. He used Augustea Inline for headlines and initial caps, and ITC Garamond for text. Some captions were on aluminum plaques of different sizes, mostly 1½" high by 4" wide.

It was ironic that a photomural 14' long and 12' tall of the last roofstone being put in place on the National Museum of Natural History in 1911 was the last thing you saw as you left the exhibit. With the completion of the museum, the artifacts from the Exploring Expedition had a resting place but not really a home. The exhibit Richard Molinaroli designed for the Smithsonian gave these artifacts a home, even if not permanently.

The designer worked with a budget of $800,000 for fabrication and installation, which did not include salary for the Smithsonian staff.

11.

COLLECTIONS IN SEARCH OF A MUSEUM

Without a federal museum, the government was ill-equipped to handle the beautiful collections brought back by the Exploring Expedition and originally intended to turn them over to private institutions. Powerful proponents of a national museum arranged instead to install the Expedition specimens in the newly completed Patent Office building, which ended up serving as an unofficial national museum for a decade and a half. The exhibits in the cases on either side of this column are typical of those displayed in the "National Gallery" of the Patent Office.

12.

Client: Office of Special Exhibits, National Museum of Natural History, Smithsonian Institution (Washington, DC)
Sponsors: Smithsonian Institution; ARCO
Design firm: Miles Fridberg Molinaroli, Inc., Washington, DC
Designers: Richard Molinaroli (principal), Ellen Eder (graphics)
Consultants (NMNH): Dr. Herman Viola (chief curator); Carolyn Margolis (project manager); Jane Walsh (anthropology collections liaison)
Fabricator: Design and Production

9. Show title designed by David Fridberg.
10. Carved Fijian figures in central case. Wall cases in this room are set in corners, breaking up room's boxiness.
11. Set on plexiglass supports, model of Expedition flagship seems to float on world chart mounted behind it.
12. Text screened on partition. Headline is Augustea Inline; text is ITC Garamond.
13. Scientists and Sailors Explore Antarctica section had deep blue wall color, reminiscent of the sea.

13.

Westwood Pharmaceuticals
Trade Exhibit

Westwood Pharmaceuticals has been selling its products to dermatologists for a long time, since the American Academy of Dermatology was first founded, and it began to feel that the profession perceived it as an old-line company perhaps mired in its ways. Westwood wanted an exhibit it could take to trade shows to brush up its image— to show its customers that it is committed to research, to improving its products and developing new ones. It also wanted an exhibit that could be changed yearly as products changed.

The exhibit that Design For Industry of Buffalo, New York, designed to fit into a 20′-by-80′ space has product-display areas at either end and, in the middle, a scientific theater where Westwood can demonstrate research and products and which can be used as a conference room the rest of the time. Westwood prides itself on working with dermatologists not only in developing products the profession needs, but also in offering them advice on how to run an office. For the initial show, Design For Industry provided a place for Westwood

and dermatologists to talk by scattering 10 Metro Rubber chairs from their own offices throughout the interior space. (The chairs on order hadn't arrived in time.)

The space, and indeed the entire exhibit, has a spotless, clinical, high-tech look, softened by spots of color provided by black-and-white blowups of electron-microscopic images printed on colored paper then tinted with sepia, and by curved gloss-Formica walls with subtle threadlike color bands. The designers mounted the photos on 3″ Gatorboard and floated them from pegs in front of the gloss-white walls.

Floors in each of the exhibit's three sections are either warm-gray carpet or—to take wear and tear—aluminum panels screwed and glued to plywood risers and given a textured white-epoxy powder-coating by spraying the powder onto the aluminum, bonding it electrically and then baking it on. Fluted, semi-clear acrylic panels 8′ to 10′ high form portions of the walls, letting people see that there is motion and activity inside the exhibit. In the product areas, occasional neon

tubes add color (and even a sense of motion when a fixed green neon tube snakes across a white wall). An occasional colored gel in a spotlight throws a subtle additional wash of color onto an area lighted by colored neon. Eight or 9′ overhead steel-tube Ultrabeam trusses tie the exhibit areas together and give it a high-tech look.

Seen here are two installations of the Westwood show. The first, in New Orleans, had a theatrical lighting grid suspended just overhead. The second, in San Antonio, where the ceiling height didn't permit a grid, used lights mounted on the Ultrabeam system, which has raceways for electrical wiring. Design For Industry extended the Ultrabeam system here to include a framework for a 22′-by-10′ banner of stretch polyethylene, suspended overhead "like a grand trampoline on its side," says Brion Charters, president and creative designer of Design For Industry. Black letters in a modified Handel typeface spell out the Westwood logo on the banner. On curved Formica walls in the exhibit's product

areas, the designers mounted the same logo in raised letters. And they screened corporate messages directly on the walls in Century bold or italic. For product information text, they used Helvetica. The purpose of two typefaces was to "imply a subtle difference between the science and commitment behind a product and the actual product."

Design For Industry had a budget for design fabrication and installation of $140,000 for the initial exhibit system in its New Orleans installation. For its revision in San Antonio, the budget was $98,000. The initial design and installation was spread over a period of 18 months; the revision took four months. Westwood plans to use this particular design framework for a minimum of five years.

Client: Westwood Pharmaceuticals (Buffalo, NY)
Design firm: Design For Industry, Buffalo
Designers: Jack Snyder, Gregory Meadows, Tim Dexter, Brion Charters, Linda Scarfia-Price, James Corp
Fabricator: Design For Industry

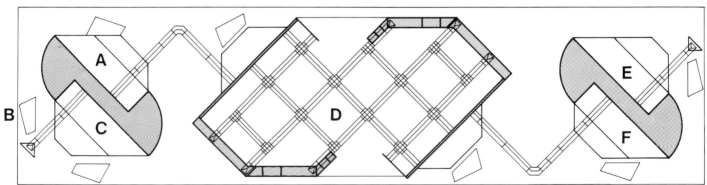

1.

Legend:
A. Product area.
B. Detail counter.
C. Product area.
D. Scientific theatre and conference area.
E. Product area.
F. Product area.

2.

3.

4.

1. Floor plan.
2. Westwood trade show Ultrabeam system holds lights and frames banner with Westwood logo.
3, 4. Within the exhibit, curved gloss Formica walls and desks display Westwood pharmaceuticals.
5. Elevation drawing.

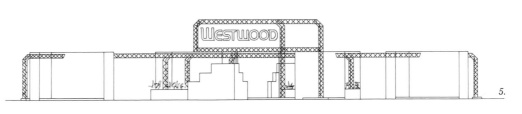

5.

Seven Ages of Woman

The Detroit Historical Museum, located in downtown Detroit across from the Art Museum, has a significant costume and textile collection. In it are some half a million items—textiles and clothing, and accessories such as parasols, fans and handkerchiefs. But until recently, the collection was kept tucked away in storage. Only a few pieces had been displayed and then hesitantly, never, for instance, given shape and form by trim-fitting them to mannikins.

The reason for this reticence was that the Historical Museum had no gallery where it could properly protect the fragile textiles and historical clothing, which disintegrate if the humidity is too high, the temperature fluctuates too much, or the lights are too intense.

All that changed when Chester Design Associates of Washington, DC, designed

second-floor space for the costume collection, giving it 6000 sq. ft. of gallery space for rotating exhibits, a photography studio, a library, preparation spaces, and storage areas for props and mannikins.

Once all that was in place, Chester Design designed the first exhibit in the new gallery (the Booth-Wilkinson Costume Gallery). Entitled "The Seven Ages of Woman," the exhibit drew on the museum collection to show how women dressed from the 1890s to the 1930s. Since the museum's collection is historical, it includes few high-fashion items, concentrating instead on "working-class and vernacular clothing." The Chester designers dressed 45 mannikins and arranged and mounted some 200 accessories. To give the exhibit coherence, they arranged it in seven sections, the Seven Ages of the title. These were: Youth, Working Woman, Bride, Social

Woman, Sporting Woman, Woman at Home, and Woman of a Certain Age. In floor-to-ceiling glass wall cases, each section showed clothing worn by women for various activities plus appropriate accessories, for instance, groupings of parasols and fans (on specially designed brass brackets painted to blend with the color of the case walls). In each showcase were one or two large items from the museum's other collections, which include industrial arts, toys and antique vehicles. The designers selected items that had some color (most of the exhibit's clothes were dark, worn in an era when dirt was a greater problem than it is today), that

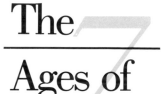

had highly articulated forms, that fit the exhibit's time niche and social categories (such as a hobby-horse or a doll carriage in the Youth section), and that showed the breadth of the museum's collections.

The biggest hurdle faced by the Chester designers in creating the new galleries was the problem of regulating temperature and humidity. A contemporary, computerized climate-control system would have gobbled most of the $250,000 budget. So, out of necessity, they worked with the existing heating and cooling system. They found new filters for the system and specified that these be changed more frequently than in the past. And by cutting troughs in the gallery floors, they ducted air directly into the new E-shaped exhibit cases. In fact, air now circulates freely through these cases, rising through the floor ducts and leaving through small gaps

1.

Mannequin Storage

Exhibit Prep

Fashion Library

7 Ages of Woman Introduction

2.

Women of a Certain Age

And the Bride Wore...

Youth

Curatorial Access / Secure Storage

Social Woman

Women at Home

Working Women

Sporting Women

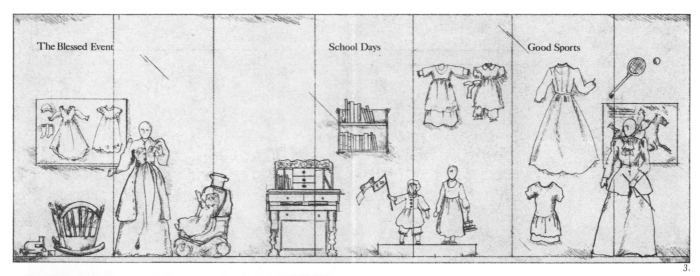

The Blessed Event   School Days   Good Sports

3.

4.

1. *Floor plan.*
2. *Show title in Bodoni Book typeface.*
3. *Sketch of wall-case. Artifacts from the Detroit Historical Museum collection are a backdrop for the costumes.*
4. *Parasols are part of the museum's costume collection.*

left between each 8'-high glass panel in the cases. Now the museum keeps the temperature inside and outside the cases, day and night, summer and winter, at a steady 69 degrees.

The lights are, of course, low voltage. Mounted on twin overhead tracks within each case (one along the inner edge, one along the outer), spotlights shine onto the mannikins and other artifacts through diffuser panels. The cases are 4½' deep and can be entered through almost invisible doors in their back walls from a 6' wide passageway tucked behind them. The overhead low-voltage, tack-mounted spotlights, however, can be changed by opening the overhead light boxes at their edges, without entering the cases. The gallery outside the cases also has twin overhead lighting tracks, though no spots were mounted in them for the first show.

Mannikins stood in the cases on rose-colored carpet. The designers covered the cases' back walls with an alabaster-colored linen, which they glued right to the plywood walls. Because a latex glue gives off a gas harmful to delicate fabrics, they used a non-acidic glue (polyvinyl acetate), and they sealed the wood before covering it with fabric.

Patricia Chester of Chester Design likes Bodoni Book type because of its "simplicity, elegance and legibility," and she used it for the "Seven Ages of Woman," as she did for "In Bondage and Freedom" at Richmond's Valentine Museum (also featured in this *Casebook*). Die-cut vinyl letters, fastened to the cases' glass panels, announce each of the Seven Ages; text captions are on a label rail in each case. This rail rises a foot off the cases' deck (which in turn is a half foot off the floor) and then slopes upward at 45 degrees for another six inches. Silk-screened on the back of a clear plexiglass 8' by 6" plaque, the captions slide into the top of the rail. Titled for readibility, these caption-plaques can be easily removed and rescreened for subsequent shows.

Probably the most formidable problem facing Chester Design was clothing the mannikins. In fact, even before they could be clothed, the mannikins posed a problem. Stored in disarray in the museum's basement, the mannikins' heads and limbs had to be attached to their torsos and then certain body measurements reduced to fit the smaller clothing worn by the smaller women of 80 or 90 years ago. A design intern worked with enthusiasm in the bowels of the Detroit Historical Museum, assembling the mannikins and spray-lacquering them. Then, the designers, curators and conservators, and a crew of volunteers fit the clothing to the mannikins, at this stage padding them in strategic places to make today's mannikins fit yesterday's clothes.

If the museum wishes, for future textile and clothing shows, it can reshape the space. The display cases are easy to disassemble. The glass panes simply lift out. Or an opaque plywood wall can be slipped into the middle of the cases to confine space, or better define it, or to cut off part of the gallery.

Patricia Chester says she was especially gratified by the enthusiasm shown by the Detroit community, which finally had a look at the Historical Museum's costumes, and by the response of costume professionals.

The designers put the galleries and the first show together in five months.

5.

6.

Client: Detroit Historical Museum
Sponsors: Booth American; Wilkinson Family Foundation; MacGregor Foundation; Matilda Dodge Wilson Foundation
Design firm: Chester Design Associates, Inc., Washington, DC
Designers: Patricia Chester, Robert Becker (detailing and construction), Yin Hoskins, Karen Ruff, Douglas Fisher (brackets and armatures), Randy Young (construction)
Consultant: Schreve-Weber Engineering (mechanical and electrical)
Fabricators: BSI

5. *Working-woman attire with labels on calf-high stands.*
6. *Bridal costumes.*
7. *Antique baby carriage and mannikins.*

7.

In Bondage and Freedom:
Antebellum Black Life in Richmond

Chester Design Associates of Washington, DC designs the exhibitions for Richmond, Virginia's Valentine Museum, a 100-year-old private historical museum. One of a series of three exhibits on the life of Southern blacks that Chester Design did recently for the Valentine, "In Bondage and Freedom," showed in an eight-month run how both free and enslaved blacks contributed to Richmond's economy before the Civil War.

The museum has a collection of artifacts used in daily work during those years, but because the exhibit was to be about people and their lives, the designers muted the display of artifacts. Instead of showing each ax, shovel, and flat iron individually, the Chester designers tied each to its human use, positioning many behind scrims on which were painted black human figures in clothes of the antebellum era. In all, the exhibit had 17 of these figures (the designers call them characters), backlighted on the 8'-by-4' scrims, posed as if using the cooking pots, mixing bowls, and tools from the museum's collection. Visitors saw these utensils and tools behind the figures, through the scrims.

Design of the characters really started with their clothes. The Valentine Museum has an extensive costume collection, and Scott Wright, the illustrator who painted the figures, drew them first in a particular costume, then checked his accuracy with the Valentine's costume curator.

Seen backlighted on the scrims in the predominantly white exhibit spaces, the figures appeared gray and shadowy by design. "We wanted them to symbolize that blacks lived in the shadowy background of the white world," says Patricia Chester of Chester Design. Besides the white of the exhibit spaces and the gray-black of the figures, the only design color was red, used for the typography.

Each of the characters on the scrims represented a particular occupation. Behind a fieldhand, for instance, was a tobacco press, used for baling tobacco leaves. A household worker seemed to be holding a flatiron. Carpenter tools were behind the carpenter, blacksmith's tools behind the blacksmith, and the barber, whose occupation was the most lucrative for a free black, seemed to be wielding a razor.

Pat Chester is quick to point out the cooperation of the Valentine curators and administrators in developing the exhibit. Usually, she says, when working with other institutions, she will be handed a script and a list of artifacts and asked to fit them all in. At the Valentine, Chester says, the staff and the designers worked as a team to develop an exhibit that became more than a static display of artifacts.

The 4000-sq. ft. exhibit held a good deal of text. The designers graded the size of the type for this text according to its purpose. For instance, all headings for sections of the exhibit were silk-screened in 2" Clarendon Condensed on panels placed up at ceiling height (8'), often between scrims. From 2" type, the size graded down through 1" and ½" (also used in headings and subheadings for overhead explanatory text), to caption-size Bodoni Book used to explain and label artifacts. This caption type was often at waist or eye level in vitrines or wall cases.

Some of the exhibit's large quantity of text appeared in books left open on pedestals for visitors to read, while copies of the catalog, hanging on chains from benches in the exhibit, gave visitors the opportunity to sit and read if they wanted to.

The amount of text to include in any exhibit and its placement are always matters of debate.

1.

1. *Figures on backlighted scrims seem to be using an artifact in wall cases behind them.*
2-4. *Scrim-painted figures of a housemaid, a butler and a family group.*
5. *Floor plan.*
6. *Field hand on scrim seems to reach for a tobacco press.*

2. 3. 4.

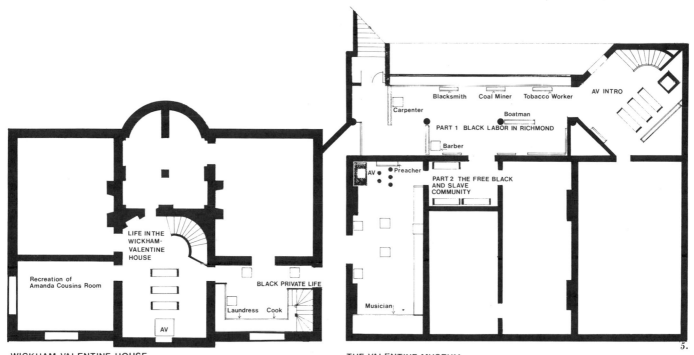

LIFE IN THE WICKHAM-VALENTINE HOUSE

Recreation of Amanda Cousins Room

BLACK PRIVATE LIFE

Laundress   Cook

AV

WICKHAM-VALENTINE HOUSE

Carpenter   Blacksmith   Coal Miner   Tobacco Worker   AV INTRO

Boatman

PART 1   BLACK LABOR IN RICHMOND

Barber

AV   Preacher

PART 2   THE FREE BLACK AND SLAVE COMMUNITY

Musician

THE VALENTINE MUSEUM

5.

6.

So is the matter of the actual wording. Research done on "In Bondage and Freedom" after the exhibit opened suggested that changes in the text might be in order, that, for instance, simpler wording might help visitors' understanding.

Funded in part by a National Endowment for the Humanities grant, the exhibit had research evaluation funding written into its NEH grant. Harris Shettel, an industrial psychologist who often works with exhibits, did the evaluation. He found that exhibit-goers, who seldom looked up, were ignoring the overhead text and headings entirely, that they rarely went through the exhibit sequentially, but rather, skipped randomly from item to item and even from section to section. Despite this seemingly skittish approach, visitors perceived the exhibit coherently. They spent most of their time with three

videotapes, each playing on a continual loop on a monitor set on a rolling cart in a viewing area with a few chairs. The video in the exhibit's first section, the one dealing with artifacts and their use, ran for 20 minutes. It was an actor's interpretation of the life of Gilbert Hunt, a local free blacksmith. The exhibit's second section dealt with the way antebellum blacks lived and worked and its video, put together by a black historian in Williamsburg, used old WPA readings about black life before the Civil War.

The third video was located at the exhibit's end, near a reproduction of some service stairs (seen through a scrim) leading from the basement exhibit galleries to the historic 1840 Wickum-Valentine house above, which is actually adjacent and connected to the Valentine museum. This final

video ran for 10 minutes and explained the significance of the house and how the black staff lived and worked in it. This video not only helped explain the household utensils in the exhibit's final section, but was also an introduction to a tour of the Wickum-Valentine house above.

The exhibit's only lighting came from overhead low-voltage spots, focused directly on whatever was being displayed. In all, the exhibit held 120 artifacts, including a lot of old prints, photos and books that needed the protection of low voltage.

The Chester designers found visitors were spending anywhere from 20 minutes to an hour in the exhibit. They might spend 35 minutes with the videos and the rest of their stay wandering around looking at the artifacts. Not surprisingly, the exhibit

attracted a mostly black audience. Visitors came from Richmond and by bus (mainly) from Washington, DC, and many of them came several times, browsing through the exhibit's reading material. In fact, "In Bondage and Freedom" was so popular that the Valentine extended its run two months beyond the originally scheduled six.

Chester Design Associates put the exhibit together in six weeks on an exhibit budget of $45,000.

Client: Valentine Museum (Richmond, VA)
Sponsors: National Endowment for the Humanities; Virginia Foundation for Humanities and Public Policy
Design firm: Chester Design Associates, Inc., Washington, DC
Designers: Patricia Chester, Timothy Priddy, Robert Becker
Consultants: Scott Wright (illustrator); Communication Design (catalog and graphics); Park Avenue Productions (videos)
Fabricator: BSI

7. Next to service stairs, household servant on scrim seems to be holding an iron.

7.

Robes of Elegance: Japanese Kimonos of the 16th through 20th Centuries

For three months in 1988, 90 kimonos from the National Museum of Japanese History in Sakura, Japan, and the National Museum of Modern Art in Tokyo were on display at the North Carolina Museum of Art in Raleigh.

The kimonos were fragile: Many dated from the 1500s and 1600s, and many had been hand-painted or woven with gold or silver threads. The Japanese were so concerned about the kimonos' fragility that they sent two curators to see that they were mounted properly and displayed in an environment that controlled the temperature to a degree or two on either side of 72 degrees Fahrenheit and humidity at no more or less than 55 to 60 per cent. When the curators departed, they left behind a representative who checked temperature and humidity throughout the exhibit's run. And because the kimonos, which are really works of art, could not stand long periods of exposure to light, the museum displayed them in groups of 30, showing each group for a month.

Meeting these temperature, humidity and lighting requirements was probably the museum design department's major problem. The museum had no money for a sophisticated computer-controlled heating/cooling system or for installing a low-voltage lighting system, so head exhibit designer Kerry Boyd had to work with what was available. He arranged his three floor-to-ceiling, glass-fronted display cases around a central core of heating and air-vent ducts, which served the entire

museum, then ran extensions from these ducts directly into his cases. But the overhead lights in the museum's ceiling-suspended grid lighting system gave off more heat then he'd expected, so he positioned lights to shine directly into the cases through diffuser panels and set up a fan and duct system to suck off excess heat. And he eliminated lights in the gallery until the only other illumination came from back-lighted shoji screens, which formed the walls of the central equipment core and extended into the cases.

Boyd wanted the feeling of a Japanese home for his cases. The shoji screens, which he had built from white pine and theatrical scrim, provided one touch; another came from raising each case off the floor in two levels, one 13″ and the other 18″, providing a sort of architectural step.

Raising the platforms brought the kimonos up to eye level, and though the kimonos on their scarecrow-like birch frames rose vertically in the cases, the shoji screens with their horizontal birch bands worked to make the exhibit seem lower.

The Japanese also sent detailed instructions for constructing the white pine stands on which the kimonos were draped along with drawings of how they wanted them draped. These stands had no screws or nails or staples, but were pegged together, and the museum built 90 of them, one for each kimono.

On the floor of each case, Boyd stretched a natural-colored linen with its outer edge held down by a 6″-wide wood

1.

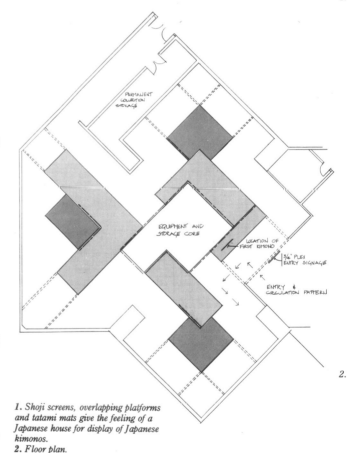

2.

1. Shoji screens, overlapping platforms and tatami mats give the feeling of a Japanese house for display of Japanese kimonos.
2. Floor plan.

strip lacquered a moss gray-green. On the other side of the cases' glass walls, an outer border of sealed and clear-lacquered white pine extended 6″. This detail extended within the cases where the two platform levels overlapped.

Captions were on wooden wedges laid on the interior strip painted the same moss gray-green. The exhibit's only color other than that of the kimonos came from this strip and from gold paint on an entrance wall where the designers screened the show title and a list of donors.

Outside, on the museum grounds, there was color. Red banners were hung on a series of PVC pipe frames to look like the sleeves of the kimonos inside. These frames marched toward the museum entrance in descending heights of 15′, 12′ and 9′. Then, on the building itself was hung a giant, vertical banner, 8′ by 26′, brown and red with the show's title in white Japanese script.

The designers carried this Japanese title inside the museum, screening it (with the English title) in white paint on a clear plexiglass panel 8′ wide by 10′ high, hung just outside the exhibit entrance and fastened so that it wouldn't swing with two metal pins running from the floor to a 6″ oak strip at the base of the plexiglass. Just beyond this panel, alone in a case, was the exhibit's first kimono, drawing you into the exhibit. When you reached that kimono, you saw more of them to your left, encouraging you to move clockwise through the exhibit.

Boyd strove to keep everything simple. "We spent

3.

4.

5.

6.

time eliminating visual noise," he says, "cutting out all extras, making it spare."

Although the designers were aware of the exhibit's arrival two years in advance and had a comfortable amount of time in which to design it, and even though they had a relatively leisurely 10 months to fabricate it and see it installed, they found enough details unfinished after the fabricators had left to keep them working day and night for three weeks before the opening.

They worked with an overall exhibit budget of $300,000.

Client: North Carolina Museum of Art (Raleigh)
Sponsors: Broyhill Industries Foundation, Inc., Hudson-Belk Stores, Mitsubishi Semiconductor Electric America, Inc., Shiseido Cosmetics, Takeda Chemical Products USA, Inc., North Carolina Museum of Art Foundation, National Endowment for the Arts, and Federal Council of the Arts and the Humanities
Design firm: North Carolina Museum of Art Design Dept.
Designers: Kerry Boyd, head exhibit designer (exhibit design), Lida Lowrey, chief designer (catalog design), Jennie Malcolm, head graphic designer (brochure, gallery guide, invitation)
Consultant: Herb Stanford, DSA Group (HVAC)
Fabricators: Michael Joerling (shoji screens), J.S. Edwards (platforms), McGee Drywall (drops)

3. Exhibit title painted on 10'-high plexiglass stands before single kimono at exhibit entrance.
4-6. Kimonos on wooden frames stand like elegant scarecrows in spare, carefully detailed setting.

Tokyo: Form and Spirit

Though it had a broad appeal, "Tokyo Form and Spirit" was quite possibly an exhibit best appreciated by designers. On display for three months at the Walker Art Center in Minneapolis were 300 examples of Japanese art from different periods, items such as ceramics, prints, lacquerware, painted screens and clothing, along with several contemporary pieces commissioned especially for the show. By showing the old with the new, the Walker's director, Martin Friedman, wanted to illustrate that art in Japan today, though contemporary in its form, textures and materials, is also deeply rooted in Japanese artistic traditions.

The art on display covered the almost 400 years since the Japanese capital was moved from Kyoto to Tokyo in 1603. It all originated in Tokyo, Japan's artistic center, where art gradually expanded from a specialized activity to something that pervaded almost every aspect of Japanese life, and in part, it is this pervasiveness that the exhibit addressed. Co-curators for the exhibit Martin and Mildred Friedman arranged it in seven sections, each having to do with a theme of Japanese city life:

- Tokyo Spirit
- Walking
- Living
- Working
- Performing
- Reflecting
- Playing

In an introductory section, in vitrines and cases, were examples of objects from the Edo (the old name for Tokyo) period. In 1603, when little more existed at Edo than a castle and some feudal rice paddies, the capital moved there from Kyoto. In 1868, the name changed to Tokyo. There were maps in this introductory space and 19th-century photographs of the city and its people.

Today, of course, Tokyo is the cultural center of Japan, crowded with eight-and-a-half million people, bustling, colorful, and exciting. The exhibit reflected a good deal of the excitement, but it showed calm, too, and by juxtaposing old art with new, it let visitors see how the old forms and traditions are very much a part of the present.

The Friedmans commissioned 11 well-known Japanese architects, artists and designers to create works for each of the seven exhibit sections. By assigning a concrete representation to each section's abstract theme, they gave the Japanese creative people something around which to organize their designs. For instance, Tokyo Spirit was represented by the column; Walking, by the street; Living, by the house; Working, by the factory; Reflecting, by the temple, and Playing, by the playground.

The Japanese designers worked mostly in teams, a designer with an architect or an architect with an artist. Each team designed something for a particular theme and a particular room in the museum. "We asked the architects and designers to make romantic and conceptual statements about Japanese culture and its continuity," Martin Friedman notes.

What emerged were as much

1.

2.

environments as works of art, and they filled the Walker's galleries without the need for any supporting exhibit design.

These environments, paintings, and constructions represented the new, or possibly the future, while objects, prints and screens, from a time when Tokyo was Edo, displayed traditionally in cases, were the old. Each exhibit section had a little of both, usually in separate areas.

You entered the exhibit past a traditional Japanese Shinto shrine gateway or *torii*. In the first gallery, Tokyo Spirit, six three-dimensional columns or towers created by Fumiko Maki were surrounded by a series of painted scrolls, huge wall hangings by Kiyoshi Awazu. Visitors could walk among the towers, each taller than a human. Maki says that his highly articulated columns— one sheathed in mirror tiles, one a model of a city wrapped around central spires, one a staircase ascending within a column, and so on—represent "the people, trees, buildings, the entire city." One of Awazu's scrolls shows a hazy white column emerging from a dark mass. It represents, he says, "an uncertain image of the future."

In the next section— Walking—artist Tadanori Yokoo created seven wall murals, each 8′ square, silk-screened on ceramic tiles. In front of each mural stood an architectural framework designed by Arata Isozaki. Artist and architect decided on one mural and one framework, depicting the city as seen while walking its streets, for each of seven historical periods, including the future.

1. Torii (Shinto shrine gateway) made especially for entranceway to exhibit.
2. Floor plan.
3. Lacquered red columns, fabric-covered walls and modular glass table on floor of crazed glass rectangles are a contemporary interpretation of a traditional Japanese teahouse in the Living section.
4. Tile painting framed by a collaged structure from the exhibit's Walking area.
5. Column composed of shrine and tower elements from the Tokyo Spirit section.

Easily the most moving mural was one denoting Tokyo burned to the ground after World War II, its river running red, and at the top of the mural, four burned, scarred hands. At the beginning of this section is a group of decorative Edo shop signs representing a pharmacist, a brushmaker, a textile dyer and other tradespeople.

In the Living gallery, a teahouse with tea-ceremony objects, bamboo blinds and rice mats, contrasted with a high-tech representation of this traditional Japanese institution, the teahouse, designed by architect Tadao Ando and designer Shiro Kuramata. The familar *tatami* (straw mat)-covered floor had evolved, in their high-tech version, into a platform of crazed glass rectangles with a stainless-steel column rising from them. Other allusions to traditional Japanese interiors in the "tearoom for tomorrow" were a row of red lacquered columns, a glass chair and, on the walls, polymer-hardened draped fabric and a hologram of bamboo shoots.

Benches in the Working area let visitors sit to watch glittering images of men and women move on acrylic panels. Computerized light-emitting diodes embedded in the acrylic traced out human forms, whose outlines and colors changed steadily through a 12-minute program. The robot-like faces and forms were the work of Hiroshi Hara, a professor at the University of Tokyo. Hara says that his images came from diagrams of robotic equipment used by Seiko to assemble watches. "I call the images robots," he explains, "but

this doesn't necessarily have negative implications. People and machines can no longer be totally separated. . . . Tokyo is like this, too. It is a city where there are no real distinctions between living and working areas." Hara placed 20 of these panels in a darkened room before a grove of geometric trees with stainless steel trunks and half-circle crowns carrying astrological symbols.

Probably the most popular area was the Performing gallery, where architect Arata Isozaki and designer Eiko Ishioka positioned 60 television screens looking up through a glass-topped stage 15′ square.

On the screens, Japanese television commercials played continuously. This stage sat on the gallery floor in front of a U-shaped space meant to evoke that of a *himorogi*, or shrine. In it was a stack of four video monitors. During the exhibition, dancers and musicians often performed on the glass-topped stage as part of the Walker-sponsored Tokyo Arts Festival. In the historical section of this space were puppets, musical instruments and Kabuki theater costumes.

To enter the exhibit's Reflecting section, you stepped through the cutout silhouette of a Buddha and passed a group of

Edo religious objects, shown via traditional museum methods. Then you moved on to the environmental space designed by architect Toyo Ito and designer Kohei Sugiura. The attempt there, Sugiura says, was "to erase from people's minds the limitations of the space and to create the impression of infinity." Part of this impression was created with mirrors, which lined the walls. Part of it came from the red scrim-covered, back-lighted floor across which you walked on a bridge of geometric panels, representing the four natural elements—a square of earth, a circle of water, a triangle of

6.

wind and a half-circle of ether. Lights flickered through the red scrim in the darkened room; the effect was of calm and quiet. Says Ito, "We wanted one to have the feeling of being wrapped in something soft."

A visit to the exhibit's last section took you past cases of Edo-period toys, games and hand-decorated playing cards, through a corridor lined with colorful kites, to the Walker's third-floor outdoor terrace. There stood graphic designer Shigeo Fukuda's giant, angular, three-dimensional wooden dog, *inu hariko.* You could look into it through peepholes and see optical images which showed that not everything is as it seems. Depending on which hole you looked through, and thus the angle from which you were viewing one of six objects, a violinist became a pianist, or a sunburst became a hand holding a cup of coffee, and so on.

For all labels and text panels, the Walker used Univers typeface, as they do for every exhibit, setting the type in the museum and sending it out to be silk-screened.

In all, the exhibit filled 17,000 sq. ft. at the Walker, and it seemed to delight everyone. In its three-month stay it attracted more visitors than any other exhibit held at the Walker save one: A Picasso show in 1980 drew 225,000 visitors. "Tokyo: Form and Spirit" recorded 204,768.

Budget for the exhibit was $1,200,000.

7.

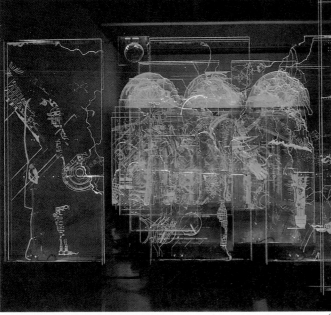

8.

9.

6. In the Reflecting area, a walkway of geometric forms lead across a scrim-covered floor through which lights flickered, reflecting on the mirrored walls.
7. Walking gallery.
8. Shapes etched on transparent acrylic layers seem to move as diodes embedded in the acrylic flicker on and off in the Working section.
9. The Playing Section's giant, three-dimensional wooden dog, Inu Hariko, *was located on the museum's third-floor outdoor terrace.*

10.

Client: Walker Art Center (Minneapolis)
Sponsors: Major funding from National Endowment for the Humanities, First Bank Minneapolis, Honeywell, Inc., SONY Co. Ltd., Japan-United States Friendship Commission, the Japan Foundation
Design firm: Walker Art Center
Designer: Mildred Friedman
Fabricator: Walker Art Center Exhibition Installation Dept.

10. Exhibit's Performing gallery with live performer on glass-topped stage. Stage held 60 TV sets on which Japanese commercials appeared.
11. Performing section includes stage with TV sets showing through glass top, black rice straw walls, triangular bamboo ladders, and a plaited rope.

11.

The Art of Micronesia

Tom Klobe, director of the University of Hawaii Art Gallery, arranged 100 Micronesian artifacts in 4′-by-8′ cases for a month-long exhibit in the 4200-sq.-ft. gallery. The octagonal gallery has floor-to-ceiling windows on all sides, and so, because these artifacts were sensitive to natural light, Klobe covered the windows with a modular wall system he built in the late 1970s, when he first became gallery director. Then he painted these created walls a light blue to represent the world of sea and sky that is Micronesia, 2000 tiny islands scattered across an area the size of the U.S. in the North Pacific Ocean.

Subsisting in four archipelagos—Kiribati, the Marshall Islands, the Caroline Islands and the Northern Mariana Islands—Micronesians have long traded and made war with one another, and the cultures of the four groupings are similar. Klobe organized his exhibit by themes such as the sea, transportation, religion, shelter, and personal adornment. It was the kind of exhibit in which the artifacts have qualities of color, texture, form and proportion that make them art and Klobe displayed them as art, grouping them in the cases to best bring out their beauty. Then, to explain their everyday use and importance, he had some of his students put together a seven-minute slide show which played in an alcove behind the entrance wall. The slides illustrated how some of the clothes were worn and the artifacts used.

Within the gallery, his cases, arranged in L-shaped configurations, became the setting. He designed them with sloping tops and open bases, suggesting the architecture of Micronesian huts. His movable, 4′-by-14′ gallery walls became case ends, and he painted them two shades of muted green. The sloping tops and case platforms were an olive green, hinting at the feeling of a Micronesian village against the "horizon" of the gallery walls.

2.

3.

1. Drawing of exhibit in place.
2, 3. Cases in L-shaped configurations have sloping tops and open bases.

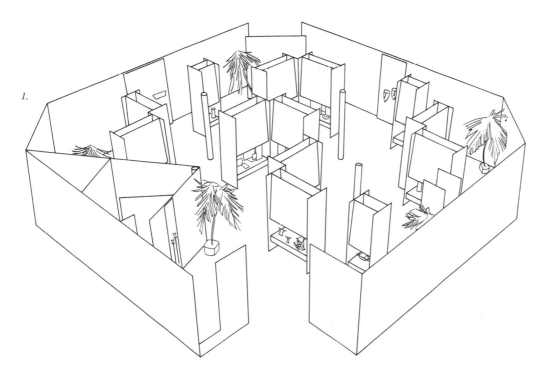
1.

It was only a hint because the artifacts from sun-drenched Micronesia had an exhibit-controlled light level of 15 foot candles. All the artifacts needed, though, was a hint. There were maternity mats, masks, storyboards which aided the retelling of important myths and histories, a female fertility figure and supporting posts from a central village meeting house.

Klobe photocopied text in sepia tones and displayed it on hanging panels 16″ wide and as much as 5′ high (their top portions obscured by the top of the cases), which he strung on monofilament line from metal bars in the cases. For this text he used Times Roman typeface. With pin clips, he also mounted photos, drawings and paintings on the panels.

Individual items in the cases bore labels typed on paper painted the same olive green of the case interiors and glued to ½″ plywood.

You could see through each case to the exhibit beyond, so there was a feeling of intimacy. Moreover, because of the subdued lighting and muted colors behind the richness of the artifacts' textures and colors, the exhibit had a feeling of stillness and elegance.

Klobe put the entire exhibit in place in three weeks with student and volunteer help on a budget of $72,108, which included publications, shipping and insurance.

Client: University of Hawaii Art Gallery (Honolulu)
Sponsors: National Endowment for the Arts, Hawaii Committee for the Humanities, Mobil Oil Micronesia, Inc., Bank of Hawaii, Continental Air Micronesia, School of the Pacific Islands, Inc.
Designer: Tom Klobe (gallery director)
Consultants: Karen Stevenson (exhibition consultant), Karen Thompson (associate gallery director), Jeanne Wiig (faculty assistant); Deborah Waite, Gerald Feldman, Donald Rubinstein (curators), Karen Stevenson, Delmarie Klobe, Donald Rubinstein, Jeanne Wiig (catalog editors); Allen Hori, Christine Kehlor (catalog designers); Peter Salter (faculty catalog advisor); Karl Miyajima, Scott Tome (audiovisual program)
Fabricators: Student gallery assistants: Scott Katano, Thomas Tsuhako, Sheryl Saito, Dean Myatt, Wai Tak Yan, Man To Wan, Florencio Paraon, Anovale Lulu, Teresa Ho-Turco, Michaela Gillan

4, 5. Visitors could see through each case to the exhibit beyond.
6-8. Artifacts were displayed as art, each with its individual space, but linked in compositions that brought out their form and color.

4.

5.

6.

7.

8.

The Art of Polish Posters

For almost a month, these posters from Poland enlivened 4,500 sq. ft. in the University of Hawaii Art Gallery. In all, there were some 200 of them culled from a collection given to the university's Department of Art by a language professor, Dr. Henri Niedzielski, who started collecting them while teaching on a Fulbright grant at the University of Crakow from 1972-74.

All of the posters were produced in postwar Poland, mostly during the 1950s, '60s and '70s, and the setting which gallery director Tom Klobe designed for them was simple and symbolic, establishing a mood that was at once solemn and joyful, like a priest dancing, but a mood also somewhat chaotic and disoriented, evocative of the mood of postwar Poland.

What Klobe did was take 40 sections of the gallery's modular wall system and arrange them spontaneously throughout the space, some tilted toward one another, some slanted away,

some angled slyly toward others. Klobe had the freedom to position his panels so randomly because the gallery has an 8' grid of eye bolts fastened into the concrete ceiling and sticking through the dropped ceiling beneath the concrete. Originally meant to hang sculpture, the bolts held, for the poster exhibit, 12' lengths of 2"-diameter, hollow, square-metal bars which Klobe slid through the bolts. Brackets fastened to one end of the wall panels slipped over the metal bars; the panels' other ends rested on the gallery floor.

These wall sections measured 4' or 6' by 14', and Klobe and his volunteer help painted them a warm, dark gray. The gray Klobe selected served several purposes. It made an ideal backdrop for the brightly colored posters, enhancing their vitality; it was also a symbolic reminder of the somberness of war-ravaged Poland and the collective state of mind which gave birth to these posters; and finally, Klobe says, the gray "expressed the elegance of Old World Poland."

Klobe worked from a model, but when he and his student gallery-assistants started installing the show, they did not follow the model exactly, but changed the panel placement around almost by whim, giving the final environment what Klobe speaks of as more spontaneity. The same procedure worked for positioning the posters on the panels. Nothing is lined up. Posters are juxtaposed for their color and form, not for their content, although they were grouped thematically, e.g.,

2.

3.

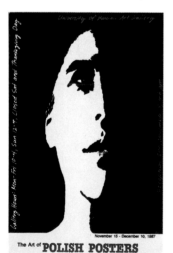

1.

motion pictures, politics, or by graphic technique (for instance, posters in one group have photographs worked into them). Instead of giving each poster a caption, Klobe merely labeled each thematic section, silk-screening the label right on a wall panel in Serif Gothic bold.

The way the wall panel sections were skewed and twisted added a sense of innovation and exuberance to the exhibit. Innovation and exuberance showed up in Polish poster art only after several postwar years in which posters had somber colors and rigid state-dictated images meant to encourage the rebuilding of the state. But as years passed, colors grew brighter and images less rigid, until in the 1960s a group of artists persuaded an official to let them produce movie posters that used freer design, working toward visual metaphor that captured the essence of a film. According to at least one authority, as this freedom took hold, Polish society began to think of poster design as an art form like painting, and today signed posters are often displayed in the same galleries with watercolors and oils.

Klobe designed the exhibit and then took a week to install it with the help of student and volunteer labor. He worked on a budget of $1615 for design and some $350 for installation.

During the exhibit the music of Chopin played in the gallery.

Client: University of Hawaii Art Gallery (Honolulu)
Designer: Tom Klobe (gallery director)
Consultants: Karen Thompson (associate gallery director, researcher); students: Thomas Tsuhako (graphics and announcement designer), Sharon Tasaka (gallery management assistant), Jeanne Wiig (color and design)
Fabricators: Student gallery assistants: Scott Katano, Malia Van Heukelem, Carla Tam, Robert Shintani, Florencio Paraon, Velma Yamashita, Monica Bacon; student volunteers: Wayne Kawamoto, Lisa Yoshihara and class members of Art 360 (Exhibition Design and Gallery Management)

1. Exhibit poster is a poster within a poster.
2, 3. Both the display panels and the posters on them were arranged to give a feeling of spontaneity.
4, 5. Display panels slant and twist to match the exuberance of some posters.
6. Drawing of the exhibit makes it look like the set of an Expressionist movie.

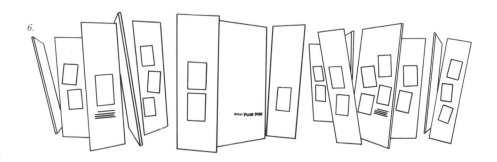

Chicago Architecture 1872–1922: Birth of a Metropolis

The exhibit framework that Stanley Tigerman (of Tigerman, McCurry, Architects) designed for a display of drawings, plans, models, and details of Chicago buildings designed by Chicago architects betwen 1872 and 1922 filled 16,000 sq. ft. of the Art Institute of Chicago during the summer of 1988. By using details and colors of the city's architecture in his design, Tigerman evoked its mood, character and design antecedents. His exhibit framework was sometimes playful, sometimes grand, sometimes nostalgic, and it was often complex, but it still managed to enhance the artifacts without overpowering them. Tigerman's exhibit framework had so many distinctive details—columns, atriums, trellises, beams, even lampposts and an evocation of the Michigan Avenue bridge— that by auctioning them off once the exhibit closed, the Art Institute put $40,000 back into its coffers.

John Zukowsky, curator of architecture at the Art Institute, initiated the exhibit. And because many of the early Chicago architects came from Germany or trained at the Ecole des Beaux-Arts, the influential architectural school in Paris, Zukowsky sent the exhibit's artifacts abroad for display in Frankfurt and Paris before it opened in Chicago. Tigerman saw the European installations, and he spent some 18 months shaping his vision of the Chicago installation, working on studies and discussing them with Zukowsky. Originally, the exhibit had been slated for a different space in the Art Institute, but once the space was set, the exhibit design, says Tigerman, "sort of fell into place."

The exhibit filled an area longer than a football field and about a third as wide, and Tigerman arranged it so that it had two long spines. Visitors passed through the length of the space, then doubled back on the other side of a central partition and left the way they came in.

You entered the exhibit down a wide staircase past two large trees flanking the lower steps, then past desks framed by columns where you could pick up an audio tour, narrated by Tigerman and Zukowsky. From the bottom of the steps, you could see the length of the exhibit, 350', past a model of Chicago on 12 pedestals, each supporting a charred block of the city the way it looked after the Chicago fire of 1871, down a central-colonnaded corridor to a 4' by 4', brightly-lighted photo portrait of Frank Lloyd Wright's head and shoulders in a curved wall niche.

The columns of the colonnade changed shape and color as you entered different sections. In the first section after the fire model, sheathed in trellises, classical columns (with what Tigerman calls "hot Tuscan colors" on their bases and capitals) and (along the wall) pilasters displayed work of architects who rebuilt Chicago after the fire. Many of them were Germans—Dankmar Adler and Peter J. Weber, for example—who had come to America in the mid-19th century. The trellises threw shadows on the framed material on the walls, "like," says Tigerman, "the entrance to the American Academy at Rome."

The second major space is devoted to models and drawings of architects who, though less known than their more famous contemporaries, produced much of the city's fabric, such men as Edward H. Bennett, Edmund Krause, Richard Schmidt and Arthur Woltersdorf. At one side of the

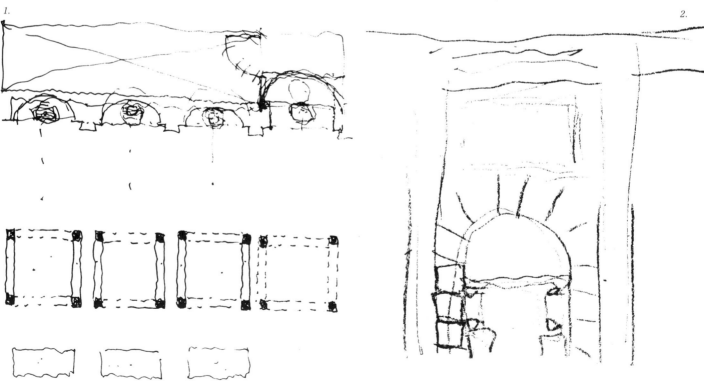

1.

2.

Photos by © Bruce Van Inwegen

space is a floor painting of Graceland Cemetery, where many of these Chicago architects are buried. Set amidst a frame of square columns and low rectangular benches, the painting's four edges carry quotations from the four masters of Chicago architecture: "Make No Little Plans" (Burnham); "Nature of Materials" (Wright); "Form Follows Function" (Sullivan) and "Less Is More" (Mies). A jazz funeral march played from wall- and ceiling-mounted speakers in a style Tigerman describes as somewhere "between Chicago jazz and New Orleans."

The exhibit space was awkward because a curving staircase cut it in two. However, Tigerman turned this intrusion to profit by tucking four kiosks, in the style of each of the four master architects, beneath the staircase, transforming the space into the museum shop.

You passed this shop after leaving the major and minor masters' space and its jazz on the way to a long gallery devoted to Louis Sullivan. Entered through a small chapel with a life-sized photo of Sullivan, the gallery was lined with pillars and pilasters (their capitals and bases light green and topped with Romanesque arches), giving it the feel of a cloister or a chapel. Besides drawings and plans, the gallery held a pair of doors from Sullivan's (now demolished) Chicago Stock Exchange, and eight Sullivan pencil sketches of ornamental details.

From the Sullivan space you saw, on a platform ahead, the dining room chairs and table Frank Lloyd Wright designed

3.

4.

for the Robie house in Chicago. Models and sketches of Wright's work and pieces of stained glass and terra cotta panels from his buildings surrounded the dining room, beneath reddish-brown Wrightian ceiling beams. Beckoning just beyond was the 4' close-up photograph of Wright.

At Wright's photo, the space carried you to the right, and as you turned you saw, some 20' away, a similar brightly-lighted photo of Daniel Burnham. This led you through a U-turn into three more galleries that stretched back toward the exhibit entrance.

In Burnham's gallery, the

1, 2. Stanley Tigerman's early exhibit sketches.
3. On floor in foreground is Burnham and Bennett's 1909 plan for Chicago. At end of colonnaded Burnham gallery is Daniel Burnham's photo.
4. Kiosks designed in forms used by four great Chicago architects—Burnham, Wright, Sullivan and Mies—stand in exhibit's sales area.

columns were classical, denoting, says Tigerman, "the power of classical language," which Burnham espoused, and the colors were polychrome. On the walls were framed drawings and paintings of Burnham's work, including a huge oil of the 1893 World's Columbian Exhibition, whose scheme Burnham designed. On the floor, painted in *trompe l'oeil*, was Burnham's and Edward Bennett's 1909 plan for Chicago. Among other things, their plan widened Michigan Avenue and the Michigan Avenue Bridge, so it was appropriate that in the exhibit's next section, a smaller, more dimly lighted room, you walked over a model of that bridge, across a Chicago River painted green on the floor. In the room's four corners were models of the four major buildings which define that location: Tribune Tower, the Wrigley Building, Stone Container Building and 333 N. Michigan. Specially made for this installation, the lightweight models were suspended on monofilament from the ceiling. Interior lights, focused downward through the bottom of the models, shone on their respective floor-mounted floorplans.

In the next gallery were drawings from the 1922 international competition to choose the firm that would design Tribune Tower. Displayed were drawings of the winners, Raymond Hood and John Mead Howells, along with those of another 30 of the 270 competition entries. Tigerman presented this gallery as an urban promenade with lampposts (designed by him)

5.

6.

7.

8.

and wooden benches lining a central walkway. Through 1'4" slits in the wall you could look through to the Louis Sullivan Gallery.

At the end of the urban promenade, you entered a space that capped the Tribune Tower competition like a T. In it were design drawings of the competition's acclaimed runner-up, Eliel Saarinen. At one end was a life-sized photo-blowup of Saarinen and at the other end, an 8" slit opened a view through to the photo of Louis Sullivan. As you left the Saarinen chamber, a guard directed you past the museum shop and back through the first part of the exhibit to the entrance.

Tigerman's design for the exhibit included everything from concept to coordination of fabrication and installation. Built off-site, the exhibit with all of its full-size columns, arches and trellises was brought into the Art Institute and put up by the museum staff, and once in place, painted.

Tigerman specified Times Roman typeface for labels and captions. He worked with an overall budget of $300,000.

9.

Client: Art Institute of Chicago
Sponsors: National Endowment for the Humanities, National Endowment for the Arts, Illinois Humanities Council, Queene Ferry Coonley Foundation, John D. and Catherine T. MacArthur Foundation
Design firm: Tigerman, McCurry, Architects, Chicago
Designer: Stanley Tigerman
Consultant: Tom Melvin (*trompe l'oeil* painter)
Fabricator: Walnut Custom Homes

5. Just beyond exhibit entrance is model of Chicago after the fire, on 12 pedestals.
6. Lampposts (designed by exhibit designer Stanley Tigerman) and benches form an urban promenade in center of gallery devoted to entries in the Chicago Tribune Tower competition.
7. Frank Lloyd Wright's dining-room furniture for the Robie House on pedestal in exhibit's Wright section.
8. Looking down colonnade in Sullivan section to Robie dining room.
9. Louis Sullivan section.
10. Floor plan.

10.

The Historical Context	*European Foundations*	*Major and Minor Masters*	*Museum Shop*	*Louis H. Sullivan*	*Frank Lloyd Wright*

Entrance

Wheelchair Access — *The Magnificent Mile* — *Daniel H. Burnham*

If pressed, you'd have to concede that David Strong knows Seattle. After all, he grew up in Seattle, studying design there at the University of Washington, and then for the past 30 years working in town as a designer—since 1968 out of his own office. He knows that Seattle holds proudly to its frontier image, that most people there don't like things too flashy or showy or smacking of big-city ways. But when it comes to design, he says, "We're all competing with Disneyland. Everyone sees that. And it sets a standard for exhibit design. You have to do something that can hold up in that light or people are not impressed."

The other time the executives of Wright Runstad & Co., a Seattle construction and real estate firm, had asked Strong to design an exhibit they could use to help rent one of their buildings, they were hesitant about the approach Strong suggested. But the exhibit he designed then worked well and when they approached him again to design the exhibit seen here, to help rent a building they were putting up at 1201 Third Avenue, Strong recalls that no one was talking about understatement.

Still, the exhibit Strong designed in three rooms on the 23rd floor of a building overlooking the site of construction work on 1201, while not understated, can not really be called overstated, either. It did have excitement and drama, and if it presented an image not in keeping with that of a simple frontier town, it was persuasive in its unstated message, which was that maybe this is the way things should be now.

Strong let the building speak for itself. The entire exhibit is the building. There is nothing else, except a few pictures of people connected with it. He displayed the building in various guises, in photographs, in drawings, in models, and in pieces of detailing and trim. Then, finally, from a window in the third and last exhibit room, prospective tenants could look out on the building under construction. The exhibit held hardly any text. Each visitors group had a guide, a Wright Runstad salesperson, who went with the group through the exhibit. And besides the three exhibit rooms, the space held a conference room and a kitchen so that Wright Runstad could have people in for lunch or dinner and then take them through the exhibit.

The exhibit really started in the entryway. There, on a 10'-high glass door leading to the foyer, Strong had a 7'-high image of the building etched into the ¾"-thick glass. Debra Caruso, a talented Seattle glass-engraver, did the engraving. By using different methods to make different cuts in the glass, sand-blasting some, cutting others by hand, occasionally using acid, she gave different surfaces within the engraving different textures, so that when Strong lighted the engraved building by placing two fluorescent light boxes behind it, one on either side and each running the height of the engraving, the building seemed to levitate within the glass. It could be seen glowing brightly as people came down the corridor toward the exhibit

1.

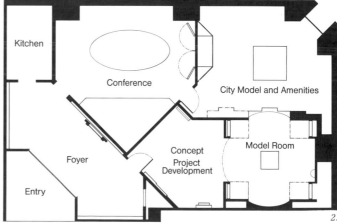

2.

1. *On left wall are models and drawings of Wright Runstad building at 1202 Third with different roof configurations. Architects set these models into a model of downtown Seattle before selecting final roof shape.*
2. *Floor plan.*
3. *Model (5' tall) stands on pedestal. In each of room's four corners is backlighted floor plan.*

S.

rooms. And it pulled visitors toward it.

The handsome and distinctive building was designed by the architectural firm of Kohn Pedersen Fox Associates, with The McKinley Architects. The architects went to some lengths to assure that the building, with its 55 stories (making it one of the tallest in Seattle) and 16,000 to 22,000 sq. ft. of office space per floor, blended into the Seattle skyline.

Strong's exhibit pointed this process out starting in the first exhibit room, where he mounted a floor-to-ceiling photo mural of a full-color section

rendering of the building as it would look when finished and covered it with a see-through early exploratory sketch of the building. "I had them empty their files," says Strong of his search for an appropriate sketch. "Fortunately, they're like me. They save everything." Once he had an appropriate sketch, Strong enlarged it and transferred it to a clear Lexan sheet, which he mounted over the rendering, so the rendering is seen through the sketch. "I like the quality of architectural sketches," Strong says, and he used sketches of parts of the building drawn right

on the wall of this first room as background for a collage of photos and sketches, showing the architects at work and some of the building's spaces. On the wall next to these photos, Strong mounted five small models of the building (from 7" to 10" high) made with what he calls "incredible detail." He glued these to a projecting wall mount and right above them fastened photos to the wall showing how the models helped them select the building's roof line. Each model had a different top configuration so the architects could place each in turn into a scale model

of downtown Seattle to see how it would look against the skyline. Photos of each model in its skyline place were displayed on the wall above the models, and above these photos were evolutionary sketches of each model.

Beyond this first or concept room, in the center of the next room, stood a 5'-high model of 1201 Third Ave. Raised on a 3' hardwood base, painted an olive gray to match the rug, the model was lighted from above. Throughout the rooms, a Lightolier system controlled the recessed 75-watt floodlighting. A Wright Runstad salesman

4.

5.

6.

guiding groups through the rooms could control the lights with a remote control, dimming the lights as he was leaving one area and bringing them up brightly over the next.

As he moved into the second room, he brought up the light on the 5′ model. Surrounding the model on two curved walls were 10′-by-10′ photo blowups of downtown Seattle with 1201 appearing completed and in place. A computer had merged images of the city taken from a low-flying plane with images of the building model. One photo showed the city at night, one during the day. Mounting the murals on the curved surface was difficult; each photo was first placed (in three sections) in a sandwich of Sintra, a vinyl-like substance that flexes without cracking. When glued to the wall, these sections kept popping loose before the glue dried. The designers had to rough up the wall surface, apply a quick-drying glue, then have four people hold the murals in place for five minutes until the bond took.

In each of the four corners of this room, they mounted one of the building's four floor plans, setting each at eye level on black plexiglass. Each plan was backlighted and the lighting controlled individually so that only the floor plan of interest to a particular group would be illuminated. At the end of the room was a wall made up of the materials and details used on the building's exterior.

As groups finished looking at the floor plans, the wall holding the night photo of Seattle slid open on floor rollers, pushed by an overhead electric motor, revealing beyond it a 7′-by-7′

city model with an overhead spot shining directly down on a model of 1201 Third. Beyond the city model, through a corner window, visitors could watch construction on the actual building.

The effect of the tour, Strong maintains, was to give visitors a feeling of being present at the building's birth. "For the first time, potential clients had a chance to understand the complex creative path required to erect such a landmark." Strong thinks, too, that the intimate knowledge given visitors made them feel involved, that if they moved in they would be "part of an historic occasion." Whatever the reasons, the exhibit achieved its purpose: Wright Runstad rented its space at 1201 Third.

Strong put the exhibit together in two and a half months on a budget of $75,000, which included everything but interior reconstruction and lighting.

Client: Wright Runstad & Co. (Seattle)
Design firm: David Strong Design Group, Seattle
Designers: David Strong, Richard Novak
Client liaisons: Steve Trainer (project manager), Jane Lantzy (project coordinator), Hamilton Hazelhurst (architect)
Consultants: Mike Jones, The McKinley Architects; Debra Caruso, D.C. Glass Lines, Inc.
Fabricators: The Graphics Co.; Lightolier

4. Backed by fluorescent lights, building image is etched in glass door leading to corporate exhibit.
5. Designer superimposed early building drawings on renderings of the building.
6. Wall in one of the exhibit rooms opens to reveal model of downtown Seattle with building in place.

AT&T Exhibit System

Until the Burdick Group in San Francisco designed this modular exhibit system for AT&T, the company's divisions used a bewildering welter of trade-show exhibition devices and designs. AT&T makes a point of explaining to customers that everything it manufactures works together, that its telephones and FAX machines and computers all interconnect, and the exhibit system the Burdick Group designed for them heightens this image of interconnecting or "networking" by doing so itself.

It consists of a series of aluminum and eggplant-colored Sintra (a vinyl-like material) horizontal floor-track sections that plug together not unlike the tracks of a model train. These tracks, which come in 2'4" sections are usually 5'4" wide and 8' long, though they can be put together to form almost any length, and AT&T divisions, which now all use the Burdick system, can set them up to suit any particular exhibit situation. The tracks rest 6" off the floor on leveling feet, enclosed in fiberglass housings.

Vertical support frameworks of steel or aluminum fit into rails on the tracks (there are three rails—two at the edges, one in the center), and on the frameworks can be hung a variety of panels, shelves, or supports in a host of configurations. Perhaps most common will be a main panel with graphics or supports for various hardware, and, above that, a rectangular horizontal panel on which text and headlines identify product groups. These panels are Sintra-covered cores. At the top of the units, a low-voltage light frame (with fixtures set in a tube) can be placed. Between the track's rails are troughs for computer and electrical cables. Using the new exhibit system, AT&T divisions, which compete with each other, can set up displays to suit any space from 200 sq. ft. to 16,000 sq. ft.

When the Burdick Group first undertook the project, Bruce Burdick (he and his wife, Susan, are the firm's principals) spent a good deal of time visiting trade shows to see what AT&T divisions were using for exhibit devices. He talked to the staff designers who had designed the systems and to the people who worked at the trade shows. He also spent time looking at the competition. Most trade-show exhibitors, he decided, build little houses, some sort of architecture to enclose their products. Burdick wanted instead something that would display AT&T products with the same sophistication and intelligence that the products themselves have, and he came up with an exhibit device which he notes matter-of-factly "is a product, and recognizable as one."

The product developed over a seven-month period of design, mock-ups, prototypes and then fabrication in Singapore, for an initial 16,000-sq.-ft. installation at the Telecon show in Geneva, Switzerland, in a joint venture with Olivetti (Milan), AG Philips (London) and AT&T (New York). From San Francisco, the Burdick Group communicated with them all by FAX. And Bruce Burdick insists it wasn't complicated.

The typeface they specified was Univers 68, because "it can accommodate a large amount of copy and still be highly legible." And in italic on the headline graphic panels it expresses "movement of data."

Budget for concept development and design of the system was $155,000.

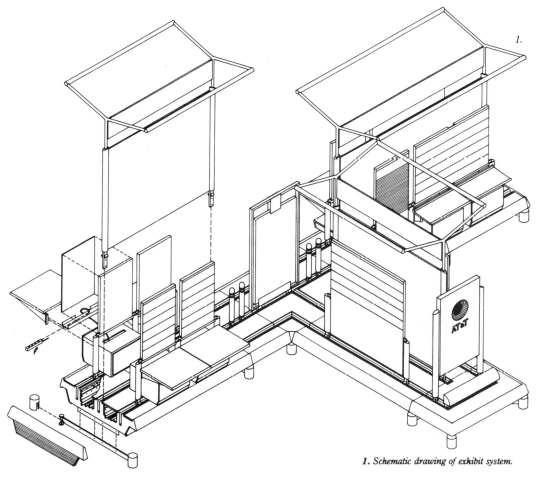

1. Schematic drawing of exhibit system.

Client: AT&T (New York City); Dick Martin, vice-president/public relations; Ron Hardaway, manager/corporate e:hibits
Design firm: The Burdick Group, San Francisco
Designers: Bruce Burdick, Susan Kosakowski Burdick, Bruce Lightbody, Marco Pignatelli, Beth Santa
Consultants: Alfred Scholze (lighting)
Fabricators: General Exhibits & Displays, Inc.; Firbank Kempster/Pico

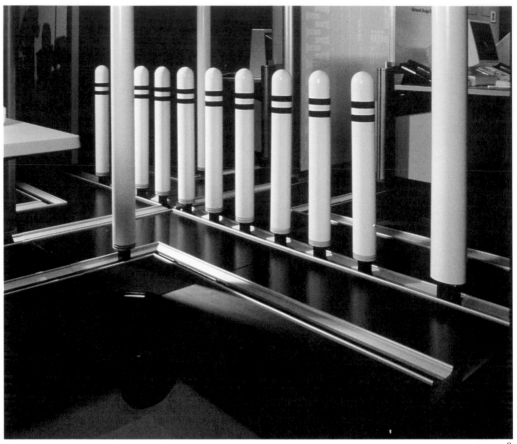

2.

2. Vertical elements reminiscent of pickets in a fence punctuate open space in the exhibit system.
3-5. Graphics and text (in Univers 68) on Sintra-covered core panels, which can be hung or placed between supports on the system.
6-8. Exhibit system can be set up in host of configurations.

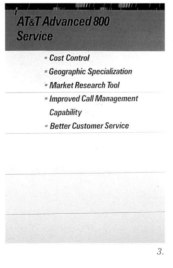

AT&T Advanced 800 Service

- Cost Control
- Geographic Specialization
- Market Research Tool
- Improved Call Management Capability
- Better Customer Service

3.

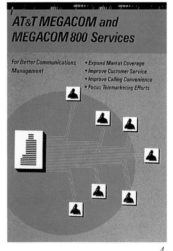

AT&T MEGACOM and MEGACOM 800 Services

For Better Communications Management
- Expand Market Coverage
- Improve Customer Service
- Improve Calling Convenience
- Focus Telemarketing Efforts

4.

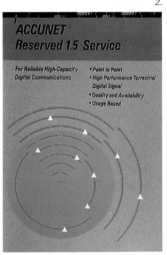

ACCUNET® Reserved 1.5 Service

For Reliable High-Capacity Digital Communications
- Point to Point
- High Performance Terrestrial Digital Signal
- Quality and Availability
- Usage Based

5.

6.

7.

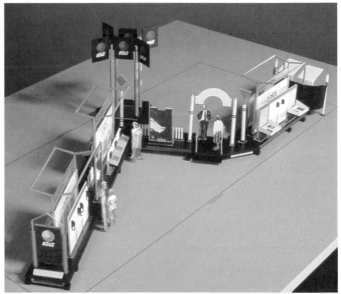

8.

Cummins Engine Company Corporate Museum

As everybody knows, Cummins Engine Company is a good design client. The company's concern for and encouragement of design has helped turn Columbus, Indiana, where the company has its headquarters, into a living architectural museum. What may not have been so clear is that the large diesel engines which Cummins manufactures are also a form of art. But de Harak & Poulin Associates, who designed the Cummins Corporate Museum, let the Cummins engines speak for themselves. The designers set the engines on stalks throughout the 4500-sq.-ft. space, and posed alone like that, surrounded only by the wood-block floors, the mirror and glass walls and the concrete columns of the Roche Dinkeloo building, the engines' artistry blossoms.

Cummins wanted a corporate museum in the corporate office building that was being designed for them by Kevin Roche John Dinkeloo Associates; moreover, they wanted the museum to present the Cummins corporate philosophy, putting it in some sort of historical perspective. And once he took on the assignment, Rudy de Harak spent considerable time travelling to Cummins plants throughout the country, asking workers what they thought should be in the corporate museum and how to exhibit the company philosophy.

The philosophy has to do with people, the not-so-arcane idea that people make the company, that people keep in perspective what the company is and where it is going. Sophistication in technology in both its application and its

1.

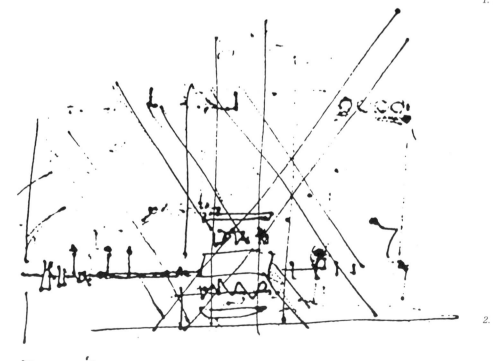

2.

3.

4.

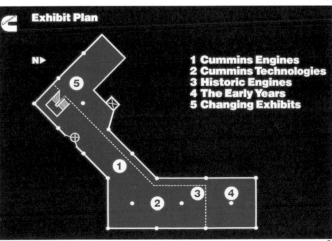

Exhibit Plan

N▶

1 **Cummins Engines**
2 **Cummins Technologies**
3 **Historic Engines**
4 **The Early Years**
5 **Changing Exhibits**

5.

1. Cummins Corporate Museum centerpiece is exploded engine, its 200 parts suspended on wires.
2. Original Rudolph de Harak concept sketch for exploded engine.
3. Cummins diesel engine stands on stalk at corporate office (and museum) entrance.
4. Camshafts and crankshafts placed vertically form a sculpture garden.
5. Floor plan.

creation has always been a point of company pride, and, of course, people are responsible for that, too.

De Harak had the luxury of deciding what he wanted to do with the museum, working out an estimate of what it would cost to design and fabricate, then using a budget based on those estimates to do the work.

Inside the front entrance of the corporate office building, in space on both sides of the reception desk, he set the museum up in two sections.

To the left of the desk as you enter is a photography table with its top canted 45 degrees, which shows and will continue to show, in rotating displays, the people of Cummins. The photos are mounted in a 24'-long glass sandwich held together by brackets. Frames for the photos are silk-screened onto the glass and can be used whenever the photos change.

Behind the reception desk is a stairway leading to a bridge which spans the first floor of the building on its way to the executive offices. If you look down from the left side of this bridge, you overlook the main museum space in an L-shaped area to the left of the receptionist. Here, the de Harak & Poulin designers planted a garden of Cummins engines, past and present, starting with the first diesel manufactured by Cummins in 1919. Shined and refurbished, these engines sprout from brushed-steel cylinders (3" to 6" in diameter) which encase steel support rods. Each steel support screws into an engine block, and its other end extends through the wood-block floor where it screws into a

LTA 10

The L10 was designed to meet the demand for a smaller, lighter-weight but still heavy-duty engine in the lower horse-power range. Turbocharging and after-cooling were an integral part of the design. The L10 set new standards for lightweight and compact size while still delivering fuel economy and quality performance. To achieve this it went through the most extensive and exhaustive test program to which any diesel engine has ever been subjected. The L10, which went into the market in 1982, is used for trucks, buses and fire trucks as well as for a variety of industrial applications.

4.92 in. bore, 5.35 in. stroke
6 cylinders
611 cubic in. (10 litres) displacement
300 maximum hp at 1900 rpm
950 ft-lb. maximum torque at 1300 rpm

6.

7.

cruciform steel mounting plate on the concrete slab beneath the floor. Information about the engines is silk-screened on the mirrored end-wall of the exhibit space in Helvetica type, a face compatible with the Cummins logotype.

Easily the museum's most stunning piece, or, more accurately, pieces, are the 200 parts of Cummins' largest diesel, suspended on stainless steel wires to look as if the engine is arrested in the midst of flying apart. Before being suspended in tension on the stainless cables (¹⁄₁₆", ⅛", and ¼" depending on the weight of the part suspended), the 200 parts were laid out in a Cummins machine shop, then fitted with specially designed drilling jigs and clamps that

disappear into the parts they hold to the cable. The cables rise to the ceiling girders (which had to be reinforced to take the weight and tension) and extend down through the wood-block floor, through the concrete slab beneath the blocks, and into the basement where the cable can be tested and retensioned by Cummins engineers once a month. From an engine approximately 4' deep, 5' high and 9' long, the separation and suspension of its parts fills a space 16' deep, 22' long and two stories high. When assembled, the engine weighs two tons, and when running, it develops 350 horsepower.

The de Harak & Poulin designers also used isolated engine parts as sculpture. A grove of camshafts and crank

shafts stands in the exhibit growing vertically out of the floor.

Color comes from a 1952 Indianapolis race car, the first to have a diesel engine, adding a spash of red and yellow to the predominantly black, white and gray exhibit. The car stands on a rectangle of bricks, a reminder of the brick track it once ran on with its Cummins engine.

Color comes, too, from two video films played at the punch of a button on stainless steel-enclosed monitors (raised on pedestals 6' off the floor). One video, three minutes long, near the Indy car, is of the car being driven at Indianapolis. The second, four minutes long, plays near four new engines and is technical, showing what a

diesel engine is and how it works.

How can you tell that the Roche Dinkeloo building is Cummins' corporate headquarters? Outside the front entrance is a bronze casting of one of Cummins largest diesels, mounted on a steel shaft surrounded by a brushed stainless cylinder.

It comes as no surprise that the museum inside effectively works as a marketing exhibit. The Cummins sales staff regularly walks clients through it, showing them the engines.

De Harak & Poulin Associates put the museum together in approximately two years on a budget of $500,000 for design and fabrication. The *Casebook* jurors called it "elegant and timeless."

8.

Client: Cummins Engine Co. (Columbus, IN)
Design firm: de Harak & Poulin Associates, Inc., New York City
Designer: Rudolph de Harak, principal-in-charge
Architect: Kevin Roche John Dinkeloo Associates
Consultants: John C. Walters/ Cummins Engine Co.; Video Communications, Inc.
Fabricators: Engineering Dept., Cummins Engine Co.; Hamilton Displays; Metalmen, Inc.

9.

6. Engine information screened on mirrored end wall in Helvetica typeface.
7. First Indianapolis racing car to use diesel engine stands on brick floor pad.
8. Closeup of exploded engine.
9. Photos of Cummins employees in a changeable photo rack. Photo frames are silkscreened on 24' glass sandwich.

Hollywood and History: Costume Design in Film

The environment designed by Dextra Frankel for 55 mannikins wearing costumes from Hollywood films reflected what one *Casebook* juror called the "flair and drama of Hollywood." She created this ambience with just a few adroit design touches repeated throughout the exhibit space, any one of which taken alone might symbolize Hollywood. Taken together, they become a sort of logotype. These elements were stairways, architectural columns and artificial palm trees.

"The first time I saw the space," says Frankel, of the 8000 or so sq. ft. in the Frances and Armand Hammer building of the Los Angeles County Museum of Art, "I knew I wanted to use staircases." Staircases, of course, are a Hollywood standby; stars are always dancing on staircases, making grand entrances down staircases, or building stairways to paradise. While staircases

would help present a Hollywood image for the exhibit, they would perform other, even more practical functions. They would offer a surface down which long skirts or trains could cascade. Raised on platforms or plinths, the stairs would elevate the mannikins and their costumes well above eye level (as high as 5′5″ off the floor) so that many viewers could see them at once. And the sides of the platforms would offer the exhibit additional wall space which could be used to mount supporting graphics.

The columns, like the stairs, are architectural and the two work well together, but the columns, given different guises in different sections of the exhibit, also provide a time reference. While the costumes displayed came from Hollywood films made over the past 50 years or so, the costumes represent almost the complete span of human history, sweeping from the Stone Age

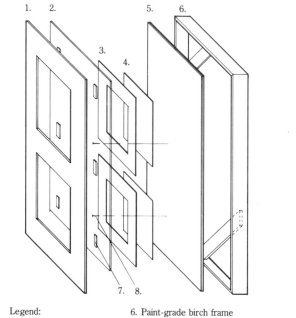

Legend:
1. ¼″ Masonite.
2. ⅛″ clear VU3 Plexiglas.
3. Nonacidic museum board.
4. Art.
5. ½″ plywood (sealed).
6. Paint-grade birch frame with diagonal supports.
7. Double-stick foam adhesive between Masonite and Plexiglas.
8. Screw through Plexiglas into plywood.

2.

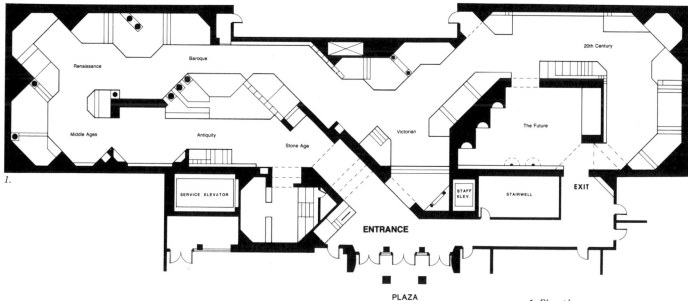

1.

1. Floor plan.
2. Exploded drawing of wall box designed by Dextra Frankel to be set in or mounted on exhibition wall to hold costume photographs. Box also serves as a shipping container.
3. Staircase-like platform raised mannikins and allowed long costumes to cascade. Columns in background were exhibit element that set time and period.
4. Wall boxes with photos set into exhibition walls.

through Egypt, the Middle Ages, the Renaissance, the Napoleonic and Victorian eras into the future of *Star Trek*. So Egyptian columns stand in the Egyptian section while, in the future section, 10'-tall columns, painted silver, taper from a wide base to 4″ or 5″ at the top.

The third Hollywood symbol, the palm tree, was designed for the exhibit by Dextra Frankel Associates and constructed out of paper. It does a better job of presenting the Hollywood image than real ones would.

Actually, there are only two or three of these palm trees in the exhibit, but they are effective. At the entrance, for instance, is a photo mural of a scene being filmed from *Garden of Allah*. In it are several palm trees and Marlene Dietrich, in riding britches and a tailored blouse. But the point is that, in front of the mural, Frankel has a short flight of stairs of the type she'll use in the exhibit to pose mannikins on. At the top of the steps is a Medieval column and at the first level of the steps is one of her paper palms.

The scene is set. A visitor gets the idea that he is entering the make-believe world of motion pictures. But the make-believe is neither excessive nor tawdry. "We wanted elegance, not glitz," says Frankel, and the exhibit was one of subdued lighting and colors. Inside the space, the designers set up the exhibit along the peripheral walls and down the center, now and then creating pockets (by angling walls) and backwaters, even forming a separate room (for the future) toward the exhibit's end, to break the flow and let visitors have more viewing space. Lighting is from

low-voltage spots and the background staircase and plinth colors are gray, in 11 different values; on the fronts of the platforms, the value is lighter than on the horizontal surfaces, and darkest of all on the walls behind the costumes.

Besides the columns and staircases, the exhibit had one other structural element, which lent it organization without contributing to its mood. To frame the graphics mounted with each costume, Frankel designed a wall box in which a black-and-white photo of each costume in use, antique fashion plates which showed what people really wore in each period, and designer sketches of the costume could be mounted regardless of their size. She designed these boxes to offer strong, coherent vertical and horizontal grids. In the exhibition at the Los Angeles County Museum, these wall boxes were inset in the walls or the plinths that hold the stairways. But for shipping to other museums where the exhibit would be displayed, the boxes were made so that they could be shipped intact, horizontally, then hung on the walls. Each box had a depth of 4″, which Frankel considered appropriate for wall hanging. In each box was a sandwich of a Masonite front, a plexiglass panel with some ultraviolet screening, a layer of museum board next to the graphic material, the art, and a ½″ plywood backing all in a birch frame.

Jeffrey Cohen, graphic designer on the Los Angeles County Museum of Art staff, selected the typeface. He used a Gill Sans, rubbing it on the

3.

4.

wall cases (using chrometeks) just below or above the graphic being labeled. He selected Gill Sans because the exhibit had a range of time periods and the face, he felt, is neutral, strong and legible.

Just inside the exhibit entrance was a small theater where a multimedia orientation show played and, at three points in the exhibit, video monitors screened clips of films set in particular historical periods. In the exhibit's last section, the future, Frankel had planned a large video projector, ceiling-mounted, to show film clips of movies dealing with that period. She wanted the projector ceiling-mounted so that it wouldn't block sight-lines at floor level. Everything was set for its installation, but when the projector arrived, just before the opening, the museum staff found the ceiling wouldn't support it. On the spot, Frankel designed a housing for the projector that would fill part of a doorway and the museum fabricated it.

Originally, Frankel had wanted to use a hologram of a spaceship floating in a beam in the middle of the floor, the kind of beam used in *Star Trek* to transport crew members from the spaceship to land. A hologram was too expensive, so Frankel, salvaging what she could of the idea, put three mannikins in futurist costumes in wall cases meant to resemble the beaming-up room on the starship *Enterprise*.

Another production hitch came from a more predictable Southern California phenomenon—an earthquake. The exhibit's period columns were designed and

5.

6.

manufactured in a complicated four-step process that saw them shipped back and forth across Los Angeles. The final stop was McGuire Enterprises in Whittier, where William McGuire finished and painted them in *trompe l'oeil*. In the midst of the column construction, McGuire's Whittier studio was severely damaged by the October 1987 earthquake and he had to move his operation before he could work on the columns.

Overall exhibit budget was $62,700. This included everything except chrometeks for labels, hand-painted entrance sign, brochure, catalog, LACMA administrators, carpenters, painters, electricians, and the work of the in-house graphic designer. The multimedia production, the film clips shown on the three video monitors, and the mannikins' wigs and makeup came from a different budget, too.

The exhibit drew material from many different sources; and it displayed costumes, film clips, sketches and photos of garments organized historically. To help the designers and the museum staff collect everything, Dextra Frankel devised a workbook, identifying costumes, time periods, film clips, fashion plates, labels, etc., by a system of numbers and letters. That way, everything could be organized by exhibit areas and ultimately laid out to see what would fit where, and what still had to be collected.

Mannikins with wigs and makeup evoked historic eras rather than the stars who had originally worn the costumes. The effect was dramatic, and

7.

8.

9.

136,000 visitors trooped through the exhibit in its 2½-month initial appearance. On weekends, as many as 4000 persons came in a day.

Client: Los Angeles County Museum of Art, Dept. of Costumes and Textiles (Edward Maeder, curator)
Sponsors: National Endowment for the Arts; three patrons of LACMA Costumes and Textiles
Design firm: Dextra Frankel Associates, Los Angeles
Designers: Dextra Frankel, Matthew Marten, Eric Gaard; Jeffrey Cohen (LACMA graphic designer)
Consultants: Amber Wilson (columns); David Inocencio/Minetta Siegel (multimedia production); Jeff Conley (installation photography, LACMA); Dan Price/Holly Film Registry (film archivist-video clips)
Fabricators: LACMA (Art Owens, project director); Paramount Pictures Corp. staff shop (columns); The French Tradition (columns); McGuire Enterprises (columns)

5. Three repeating exhibit elements—column, staircase and paper palm tree—stand at exhibit entrance.
6. Combining the repeating elements in endless heights and configurations gives the exhibit cohesiveness and variety.
7-9. Colors and lighting were subdued. The designer specified 11 different values of gray. These shaded from darkest on walls behind costumes to lightest on platform fronts.

Credits provided by the Los Angeles County Museum of Art (LACMA) are, left to right in photographs, listed in this order: movie title and/or actor wearing costume: costume designer(s); lender or other costume source. Fig. 3: Camelot; John Truscott; Burbank Studios. Fig. 4: Tron; Elois Jenssen; Walt Disney Studios. Fig. 5: Entrance to Exhibition (photographer: Jeff Conley); Caveman; Robert Fletcher; Fur lent by Bomper Furs of Beverly Hills. Fig. 6: Lois Chiles in The Great Gatsby, Theoni V. Aldredge, Paramount Pictures Corp.; Mia Farrow in The Great Gatsby, Aldredge, Paramount Pictures; Bernadette Peters in Pennies from Heaven, Bob Mackie, Lorimar Studios; boy in chorus in Pennies from Heaven, Mackie; girl in chorus in Pennies from Heaven, Mackie; Julie Andrews in Thoroughly Modern Millie, Jean Louis, Western Costume Co. Fig. 7: Jennifer Jones in Madame Bovary, Walter Plunkett, California Mart; Eva Marie Saint in Raintree County, Plunkett, California Mart; Elizabeth Taylor in Raintree County, Plunkett, LACMA; Cyd Charisse in The Kissing Bandit, Plunkett, California Mart. Fig. 8: Alice Faye in Little Old New York, Royer, LACMA; Lucille Ball in DuBarry was a Lady, LACMA; Joan Caulfield in Monsieur Beaucaire, Mary Kay Dodson, Paramount Pictures. Fig. 9: Desiree, Rene Hubert, LACMA; Marlon Brando in Desiree, Hubert, LACMA; Desiree, Hubert, LACMA; Tyrone Power in Lloyds of London, LACMA; Jeanette MacDonald in Bittersweet, Adrian, LACMA; Jeanette MacDonald in Maytime, Adrian, LACMA.

Himalayan Highlands

On three acres of New York City's Bronx Zoo, designers of the New York Zoological Society, the zoo's parent organization, created a bit of Nepal. They wanted it to be home for two dozen snow leopards and other Himalayan species, including a couple of red pandas, some Temminck's tragopan pheasants, and white-naped cranes. These animals are all found in Nepal and at the moment are all endangered species. The zoo felt it important not only to display these animals, but also to let people see the surroundings they live in, and then, given that context, to help visitors understand why the animals are endangered and why it is important that they survive.

To create the environment, the zoo moved tons of rock and soil and planted nearly 2000 trees, shrubs and grasses representing some 74 different species, almost all Nepalese.

As a result, the site has several rhododendron thickets and simulations that include a strewn mountain meadow, a scree slope with a rushing stream and a birch-shaded hillside with huge rock outcrops. To make all this as natural as possible and still keep the zoo visitors and the wildlife from getting at one another, the designers went to great lengths to hide the safety-glass panels, wire strands and wire mesh netting that form barriers within the site. They created protective barriers of rocks made of fiberglass-reinforced concrete; strung oxidized wire between viewing platform overhangs and buried steel beams, and hung netting from poles covered with carefully

sculpted epoxy bark and set behind trees.

In all, the design department created thousands of square feet of artificial gneiss and mica schist like that of the natural Bronx bedrock. To make the artificial rock pieces lighter and easier to lift into place, they molded a plastic polymer, Forton, ½″ thick, in 12′-by-8′ sections that eight men could carry easily.

In the northernmost part of the "Himalayan Highlands" snow leopard site, visitors view the cats from beneath a replica of a Nepalese bridge. Here, as elsewhere in the exhibit, the sight lines are controlled to make the steel mesh tent that covers the site practically invisible and to offer direct views of the leopards. And the landscape is arranged to get the cats close to the viewers. One

1.

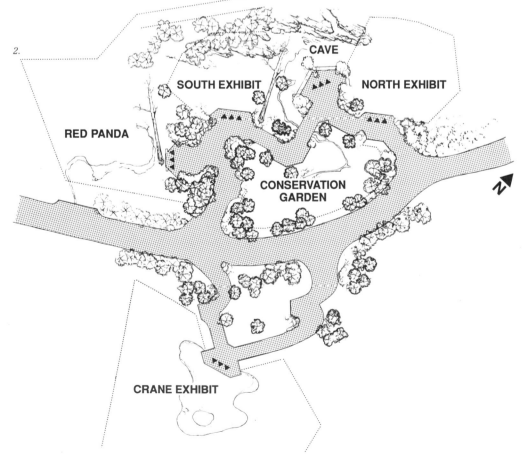

2.

1. *Artificial gneiss and mica shist molded of Forton, a plastic polymer.*
2. *Site plan.*
3. *Snow covers snow leopard site. Viewers stand beneath Nepalese-style bridge and view leopards beyond vertical wire strands.*
4. *Graphics on aluminum panels are mounted on wooden pylons capped with capitals hand-painted by a Tibetan artist.*
5. *Snow leopard viewing visitor.*

artificial rock directly in front of the viewing space has a heating coil built into it. Attracted to the rock's warmth in winter, the leopards lie on it only a few feet beyond the visitors.

In a cave area just beyond the northern snow leopard site, visitors see the cats only an arm's length away behind a sheet of glass, positioned to prevent reflection and so to seem almost invisible. The designers built a conduit to let a small stream trickle beneath the glass, carrying the sound as well as the sight of the habitat beyond the glass partition.

Although paths lead visitors through the site, which is in part heavily wooded, the designers help visitors stay oriented by positioning 6'6"-high directional pylons at 20' or so intervals throughout. They mocked up these pylons in foam core to get the positioning right before setting them in place. For one thing, they wanted the pylons situated so people would be lured on by the view of the next one, and at the same time they wanted each shaded if possible to prevent the graphics from fading in the sunlight. Graphics giving directions and other information are on aluminum panels whose edges wrap around pipe sections, which are attached to the pylons. Graphics were silk-screened on with urethane paint, then given an overcoat of clear urethane with a light ultra-violet block in it. At the top of each pylon is a capital painted by a Tibetan artist brought from Nepal. These capitals, bright with such Himalayan motifs as multicolored calligraphic prayers and Lotus flowers, give a splash of color, but otherwise

6.

7.

the graphics are muted to let the environment be the star. Graphic animal images are high-quality mezzotint photographs with the background airbrushed out so that the images seem to pop from the white colored aluminum toward the viewer. Some graphics (explaining conservation problems, scientific techniques, religion, microhabitats, animal ecology, etc.) are on waist-high panels 12″ or 16″ deep and up to 30″ or even 44″ long, set on wooden supports.

One panel, labeled "Conflicting Viewpoints," has a picture of a scientist or politician and a printed message concerning a troublesome conservation issue on three welded aluminum boxes. The boxes have a vaguely human-silhouette shape and are suspended in the panel on pins at the top and bottom, which let them flip over to expose the picture of another person on the back side with a conflicting

8.

9.

message about the best way to protect endangered species. Typeface is Helvetica with Kabel bold for titles. "Kabel is a very simple, sans-serif face," points out John Gwynne, the New York Zoological Society's deputy director for design, "and it has a rustic quality which harmonizes with the exhibit's northwoods environment."

At the exhibit's entrances, bright red Asian prayer flags catch the breeze.

The design staff worked with a budget of $1.25 million, all of which was raised specifically for the exhibit by the zoo's women's auxiliary.

One of the delights of the project for John Gwynne was watching two snow leopards "on a January day in a snowstorm bounding across rocks and rolling in the deep snow. These were no longer zoo animals on exhibit but two marvelous wild creatures who were obviously happy and having fun."

Client: New York Zoological Society (Bronx, NY)
Design firm: Exhibits & Graphics Dept., New York Zoological Society
Designers: Dr. William Conway (general director, New York Zoological Society), John A. Gwynne, Charles H. Beier, Walter Deichmann, Miloon Kothari, Ieva Vanags, Curt Tow, Sharon Kramer, Ron Davis
Fabricators: Hank Tusinski, Gary Smith, Charles Hruska, Don Williams, and in-house staff (artificial rocks and trees); Chris Maune, Tom O'Flynn (graphic production); Pat Ross, Mark Wourms, Tim Hohn, and in-house staff (horticulture); F. Gabriele, Inc. (general construction and carpentry)

6. Graphics on pylons are tucked into the environment.
7. Structures on the site have Tibetan detailing.
8. Graphic panel presents conflicting environmental opinions on swivelling silhouettes.
9. Tibetan prayer flags.

Farm in the Zoo

Within Chicago's Lincoln Park Zoo is a cluster of five farm buildings. A barn in the center of these buildings holds exhibits that explain what farming is and help visitors, mostly youngsters, relate to farming and farm animals. The other four buildings shelter such farm animals as cows, horses, pigs, goats, sheep, and chickens. Then there's a small area where it's possible to grow farm crops like corn, soybeans, peppers, alfalfa, wheat, etc.

Bedno/Bedno, Inc. devised a graphics program that unifies this farm area and gives it an inviting graphic identity. In the main barn, the firm designed exhibits which were the original assignment and out of which the graphics evolved. In fact, Ed Bedno says: "In a sense much of the exhibit *is* graphics, rather than being supported by graphics."

What Bedno/Bedno did was to distill complex subjects like agribusiness, farm management and livestock breeding to a few readily understood concepts, then commissioned some children's book illustrators in the Chicago area to prepare graphics that illustrated these concepts in images children were used to seeing. Illustrations on one panel, for instance, show a farmer leading cows into the barn to be milked, then the milk being trucked to a dairy plant where it's turned into dairy products and packaged. Next, it's trucked to the market where, in the last illustration on the panel, a child walks off with a five-scoop ice cream cone. Although they were designing with children in mind, Bedno/Bedno came up with graphics that have a

1.

2.

1. *Exterior graphics are on 1"-thick fiberglass panels.*
2. *Checkerboard floors, counters and overhead mirrors denote live-display areas.*
3. *Early farmer.*

3.

universal appeal, capable of drawing people of all ages into the exhibits and entertaining them while instructing.

Throughout the "Farm in the Zoo" are approximately 70 graphic panels with more than 170 original illustrations. In the central barn, these beige-colored exhibit panels are of ¾" marine plywood 4′ wide by 5′ tall, bolted to barn-red pipe supports 4" in diameter. Bedno/Bedno silk-screened the graphics onto the panels, then coated them with a thin laminate. Exterior panels are 1"-thick fiberglass, mounted on the buildings by hook-on brackets which keep them far enough from the walls to prevent water from being trapped or birds' nests from appearing.

The designers used little text. They specified a Charette typeface for headlines and titles because they felt it has a "down home" look. For introductory text, they used Century Expanded and for explanatory text, Futura Book. The latter two are common schoolbook faces.

The Lincoln Park Zoo had had unsettling experiences with illustrative photographs exposed over time to light and temperature differences. It welcomed the Bedno/Bedno solution of substituting cartoon-like illustrations that lend charm to the process of explaining farm operations. In fact, the zoo liked what Bedno/Bedno was doing so well that it expanded what was originally a 10-month, $100,000 program into one that backed and filled over three more years of weekly meetings, as zoo personnel changed, into one budgeted at $400,000.

Bedno/Bedno filled the central barn with exhibits you can take part in. There is a scale whose large, round, overhead readout shows you your weight next to that of a farm animal weighing approximately the same. There are panels where you can measure your height against a full-sized illustration of a goat or a cow or horse, and panels that offer you a quiz or give you unique facts about farms and farm animals.

Interspersed with the graphic panels and the interactive devices are a working beehive, a scale model of a contemporary beef farm, and live-demonstration areas. Bedno/Bedno delineated these demonstration areas, which usually have little more than some shelves, a table with an overhead mirror, a counter, or an animal pen to mark them, by giving each a standard industrial checkerboard floor of 14" black-and-white checks. In these areas, demonstrators dressed in 19th-century farm clothes show how to use tools once common on farms but seldom used now, such as apple-corers, spinning wheels, or wooden hand-operated butter churns. In an animal pen at one end of the barn, demonstrations involve farm animals. From time to time, cows are milked or maybe sheep curried. And elsewhere in the barn, someone may be baking pies, making corncob dolls or holding candles to eggs to see if they're fresh. At any one time, as many as six demonstrations may be going on at once.

At one end of the barn is a theater with benches designed by Bedno/Bedno to stack or to

4.

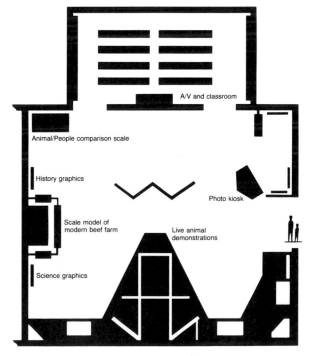

A/V and classroom

Animal/People comparison scale

History graphics

Photo kiosk

Scale model of modern beef farm

Live animal demonstrations

Science graphics

5.

6.

7.

serve as display shelves when not in use. Here, a busload of school children can sit for an extended demonstration or a film.

Except for some lights on a dropped lighting frame over the demonstration area, the barns have no special lighting. But down the ridgeline of the main barn is a huge skylight.

In 1986, while the "Farm in the Zoo" project was underway, the Bednos moved their office from Chicago to Memphis, Tennessee, so they could teach exhibit design at Memphis State University. Some of their students there were involved in design production for the project.

8.

9.

10.

11.

Client: Lincoln Park Zoo (Chicago)
Sponsor: Lincoln Park Zoological Society
Design firm: Bedno/Bedno, Inc., Memphis, TN
Designers: Jane Bedno (project director, designer, writer), Ed Bedno (project designer), Marjorie Boccio (graphics associate), Tabitha Warren (administrative coordinator), Lisa Francisco (production coordinator), Michael Guthrie (graphic production)
Consultants: Carl Kock, Donna Reynolds, Cathy Sawner, Daphne Hewett (major illustrators), John Aldridge (detailing), Pat Gulley (diorama and model-maker)
Fabricator: Design Craftsmen (Clark Swayze, president)

4. *Graphic depicts dairy business from cow to you.*
5. *Floor plan of visitor orientation barn.*
6, 7. *Graphics explain agriculture.*
8. *Agribusiness from farm to consumer on graphic panels with no text.*
9. *Children can measure their height against full sized graphics of farm animals.*
10. *Scale gives visitors' weight compared to that of farm animals'.*
11. *Take home a souvenir photo.*

Body Works

The Pacific Science Center is a private non-profit science museum on the site of what was the Seattle World's Fair in 1962. The first of the six buildings that comprise the museum was the U.S. Pavilion at the Seattle Fair, and it's in this first building that Daniel Quan of Daniel Quan Design in San Francisco designed an exhibit that fills the pavilion's 7000 sq. ft. with color, light and motion. What the Center wanted was a new, permanent exhibit dealing with the human body and health, one that would promote fitness and perhaps at the same time teach some basic physiological principles. They asked Quan for an exhibit that both adults and children could enjoy by participating in it, one that would be self-explanatory with minimal text, one that would let visitors test themselves without giving them a medical diagnosis, and one that would show people by example what they could expect from the rest of the Science Center. The fabrication budget was $180,000, to be augmented by having the museum's exhibits design department and educational staff do some of the fabrication and installation. Time from design start to exhibit opening was a scant four months, *and*, during construction the exhibit space had to remain open to the public, which used it as a way to enter the Center's five other buildings.

Quan organized the exhibit in and around five open pavilions (12′ by 12′ by 10′ high) with teal-colored support columns and yellow and white roof beams. In the center of the space he put large displays that

1.

2.

rise vertically (1′ to 20′) from the floor to above the level of the light grids, which drop from the 30′ ceiling to 14′ off the floor. Says Quan, "I wanted the light to carry up into the space." And it does, for these vertical elements are lighted with neon and flashing lights that draw attention. Even above these elements there are splashes of color. Starting several feet above the light frames, Quan hung nylon appliqué banners in the same bright colors as the rest of the exhibit, letting them extend down to about the 14′ level. "I borrowed the exhibit colors from the Los Angeles Olympics," Quan says. "They are bright, but none of them is primary." Instead, he used turquoise, teal, blue-violet, orange-reds, red-yellows and large expanses of neutral gray backgrounds. "I didn't want too much color," he explains. "It gets the kids bouncing off the walls."

Most of the construction was done with plywood and wood framing and laminated Formica, and because of the budget and time schedule, he found himself designing his participatory exhibits with at least one eye on who was going to build them. Sometimes, a piece would go to many different fabricators, each one adding something and passing it on. That this system worked at all, Quan credits to the way he and two key members of the Science Center staff, David Taylor and Stewart Kendall, were able to work closely together. The three of them became a clearing-house for the problems and scheduling of the many trades and subcontractors used to get the exhibit built and installed. A

3.

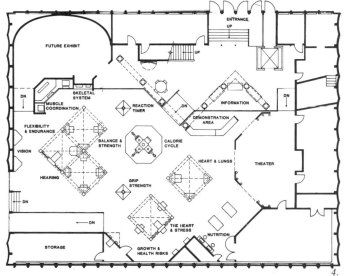

4.

5.

1, 2. "Body Works" teaches about the body through a number of self-explanatory tests that tell visitors about their balance, endurance, flexibility, and so on.
3. Exhibit is organized around five open pavilions framed by columns and overhead grids. Above these framing elements are lighting grids and banners.
4. Floor plan.
5. Logotype.

6.

7.

good part of the installation was done at night, to avoid disrupting the public passing through the site during the day.

Also, because of time and budget, Quan couldn't build working prototypes. Instead, he had to be content with cardboard mock-ups of sections of the exhibit on which he could test positioning of controls and type.

Type generally was confined to instructions, telling how to work the machines and what can be learned from them. Everything is participatory. For instance, at the base of the

drum-like canopy that dominates the exhibit on a 15'-column just beyond its entrance are three bicycles set on clear acrylic bases. Visible through the bases are the chains and gears that connect each bike to a 24" aluminum ball. As the bike is pedaled, a ball rises on a chain from the pedestal it rests on. How far it rises depends on pedaling speed. On either side of the "Calorie Cycle" is a steel rod rising 20' toward the Center's roof. Both rods carry a string of 64 lights. Those on one rod light up in sequence to show how strong your grip is.

On the other, they illustrate how fast your reaction time is. A couple of the "Body Works" devices are just as simple, but not quite as striking. To test endurance and flexibility, you hang from a chin-up bar. When your feet leave the mat, flashing lights start moving like the tip of a second hand around the periphery of a clock face. When your feet touch the mat again, the lights mark your time off the floor. To test balance, you stand on a fulcrum, a short board balanced on a central support. The handle in front of you is a switch. When you

let go of the handle, a time indicator starts moving on a clock face. When one side of the board touches the ground, the time stops.

Quan toured the U.S. and Canada checking out similar exhibits to find out what he might try in Seattle. Several of his ideas, he says, came from the Ontario Science Center, ideas which he refined and polished.

The exhibit has four computers with keyboards. In a nutrition section, you sit at a keyboard and select a meal of foods from plastic models set

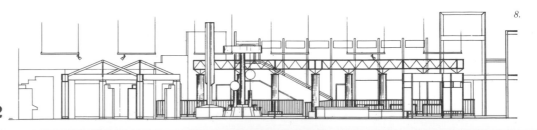

8.

out behind a counter in front of you. Video screens surrounded by the plastic foods give you information about calories and nutritional value. Another computer kiosk lets you determine how long you will live, given your particular way of life and your heredity. And an ingenious computer programmed by Ed Tannenbaum, who specializes in devising computer games for museums, lets you match one side of your face with its twin, showing you what you'd look like, say, if your face was made up of two right halves. Or you can set the computer to show you as you are seen by others coming toward you. Quan positioned the computer displays and kiosks on the exhibit perimeter,

where he kept the light softer, concentrating the brightest light on the pavilions. Also in the space is a theater with fixed benches beneath a canopy where health films not produced by the museum show every now and then. A demonstration area has books and two docents in constant attendance when the exhibit is open.

As you come in the front doors of the building, you see a white-steel truss-work running horizontally atop 18″-diameter steel culvert pipes painted a turquoise blue. These frame the exhibit space's front edge, and the trusses foreshadow a similar system in the Center's other buildings. One space meant to be in the exhibit stands vacant: The budget ran out before a sensory-

deprivation room could be designed.

Quan says he managed to meet the deadline by working day and night for four months. It's a source of satisfaction to him to have completed such a major assignment in such a short time "with virtually no budget." And he gets a kick out of seeing people using the exhibit just as he designed it.

One of the *Casebook* jurors commented on how the exhibit "literally surrounds the viewer with stimulating visual impulses." Quan managed to create a midway, a carnival atmosphere, that generates adventure and excitement. Maybe that's not a bad atmosphere in which to learn.

Client: Pacific Science Center (Seattle)
Design firm: Daniel Quan Design, San Francisco
Designers: Daniel Quan; David Taylor, Stewart Kendall (Pacific Science Center Science Dept.)
Consultant: Ontario Science Center, Toronto
Fabricators: TRSW Manufacturing, Pacific Science Center Exhibits Shop, Ed Tannenbaum (video simulator), R. Scott Productions, Eyrie Studios.

6. Nutrition section has computer on which visitors make food selections from plastic models behind counter. Information about nutrition and calories shows on video screens.
7. Reaction-time test. Lights running up the pole stop when the visitor reacts by pushing button.
8. Exhibition elevation drawing.
9. Weighing and measuring yourself against others of your age and gender.
10. Child tests her muscle coordination by pushing button that controls mechanical arms that pump bicycle pedals.

9.

10.

Cycle Composites Trade Show

Cycle Composites had a hot new product, a bicycle with a one-piece carbon fiber frame, called the Kestrel 4000. To introduce it to the world, Vance Trimble of the Brücke Group in New South Wales, Australia, designed this 200-sq.-ft. (10' by 20') exhibit for the bicycle trade show in Long Beach, California. Trimble's brother had developed the bike for Cycle Composites, a California firm, and Trimble had developed the company's corporate identity.

He knew that 200 square feet wouldn't be enough space to hold everybody who had expressed interest in the bike, let alone those who would be coming upon it for the first time. So he decided to suspend the bicycle over a pedestal at the front of the exhibit space and, in a sort of visual redundancy for emphasis and so that people could touch the product, he mounted three frames on the rear wall. He stepped this wall out in 4' sections, creating four 4'-by-8' display panels. Overhead, he built a trellis of redwood 2-by-4's, cut to look like I-beams and painted black, and hung the bicycle from it on plastic-covered steel wire. Then, to make sure the bike stayed motionless in the space above the pedestal, he anchored it by

running a wire from each wheel through the top of the pedestal to two-pound weights.

This was Trimble's first exhibition design, but he had, of course, designed the Kestrel logotype, and he made use of it here. Its red, yellow and green on one of the rear panels and on the bike frames became the exhibit's only color—except for a red light thrown upward onto the bicycle from a red neon tube running beneath it in the pedestal like a crimson gash. To "enhance the product and make it king," the exhibit's color scheme was kept to a monochrome (gray). Spotlights overhead in the trellis lighted

the bicycle and the rest of the exhibit space.

Said one of the *Casebook* jurors: "After so many trade exhibits which screamed for attention, the irony of the understatement in the Cycle Composites show was its strength."

Trimble put the exhibit together in six weeks on a $5000 budget.

Client: Cycle Composites, Inc. (Watsonville, CA)
Design firm: Brücke Group Pty Ltd., McMahon's Point, NSW, Australia
Designers: Vance Trimble, Christine Haberstock
Fabricator: Cycle Composites, Inc.

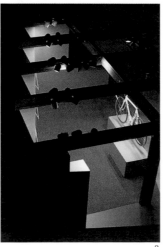

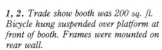

1, 2. Trade show booth was 200 sq. ft. Bicycle hung suspended over platform at front of booth. Frames were mounted on rear wall.
3. Overhead trellis held spotlights.

Hasbro Showrooms

It took about 90 minutes for a professional buyer to be escorted through the New York City showrooms of Hasbro, Inc. for the annual viewing of its toy lines. In all, the showrooms held 17 separate exhibits in 8500 sq. ft., one for each of the 17 distinct Hasbro toys, and each stop was carefully orchestrated. Each exhibit had to make readily apparent what the toy was and at the same time make it exciting for the buyer. Besides, each exhibit had to establish and maintain a Hasbro corporate look. In each exhibit, someone demonstrated how the toys worked, pitched the packaging and promotion, and saw to it that each group moved to the next exhibit on a carefully controlled schedule. The stroll to the next room, and hence the distance between exhibits, was an important design consideration. If it sounds a little like theater, it is. Thus, it should be no surprise that Don Campbell, owner and senior designer of Design Etc., Inc., the firm that designed the

showrooms, studied theater design at the University of New Hampshire in the early '70s and segued into exhibition design through the stage door.

One of the best-known Hasbro toys, G.I. Joe, has been around for a while as a military doll with a host of support vehicles and weapons. My Little Pony is a doll pony that comes in an array of colors and is collected by young girls around the world. Despite the variety of the exhibits designed for these and all the Hasbro toys, each exhibit contains a lectern or podium where an actor can stand and give a pitch explaining each toy line. And somewhere in the exhibit is a video screen where a commercial for that toy can play. The toys themselves most often stand on shelves or racks with a background that helps explain them while lending some excitement. For instance, in the 1988 exhibit, G.I. Joe dolls stood on steel-wire structures looking vaguely like space stations and on a cliff-like

structure with many plateaus. Overhead was a revolving radar-like dish, surrounded in a neon halo, and also overhead was a rocket, spewing vapor from its base. The backdrop of the My Little Pony exhibit was a setting of photo posters of children in various national dress holding the small ponies.

Obviously, each exhibit was different from the others, and to ease the transitions from one to another, or as Don Campbell puts it, "to make the transitions as seamless as possible," the designers picked a dominant color from one space to become an accent in the space that followed.

Campbell says his firm spends a good deal of time seeing that each exhibit is set up so that the message is clearly presented and can be clearly perceived. From where a viewer stands to watch a video, "is there anything that will distract him?" Is the company position on a product clear? Is it a classic line or a fad item? Somehow, in each

2.

1.

1. Hasbro showrooms had 17 exhibit settings for 17 Hasbro toy lines. Backdrop shows the Hasbro novelty dolls, B.A.B.Y., coming to earth on moon beams. Each doll is different.
2, 3. Hasbro toy duck is over 4' tall. It was exhibited in a nursery-like setting with overscale furniture and baby blocks that measured from 10" to 36".

3.

4.

5.

4. *Pipe-and-canvas pavilion holds a 2'
sneaker with a giant Tongue Tie tied to
the laces. These small (in reality) fashion
accessories appear tied to the shoes on the
mannikin feet peeking out from beneath
the canvas at floor level.*
5. *FAZZ, a Hasbro line of compacts that
attach to jewelry, were shown on hot-
colored cones, cylinders and balls.*
6. *Floor plan shows arrangement of 17
exhibit spaces.*
7. *Working kitchen displayed Hasbro line
of parent-child cooking sets.*
8. *For exhibit of "rapping" musical
instrument, Hasbro made a small exhibit
space seem larger by reflecting neon
graphics in a gray mirror, creating an
illusion of depth.*
9. *Cardboard cutout figure 5' 4" tall
represents a line of 5½" Hasbro plastic
figures, Cops 'n Crooks, based on a TV
cartoon series. Designers created a fantasy
setting with chrome vinyl floors, jail bars
and a glaring, domed overhead light.*

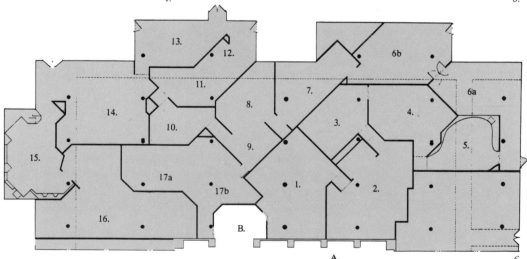

6.

exhibit, the design should say something of Hasbro commitment to the line and the industry.

In this winning showroom layout, Design Etc. had to handle the introduction of a novelty item called Tongue Ties that was around for just one summer, then pulled from the shelves. Tongue Ties were small quilted representations of mostly common things like hot dogs, tennis rackets, and roller skates that you'd tie to your shoelaces and let bounce around on your foot as you walked, "a fashion accessory" the industry called them. To display them, Design Etc. built an 8'-high pavilion-like structure of blue pipe and orange canvas. The pipes rose from two orange 4½"-high platforms. Standing on the platforms were groupings of mannikin legs whose upper reaches disappeared behind the pavilion's canvas and whose feet wore shoes, socks and Tongue Ties. Hanging from the pavilion's top was a large, 2'-high white shoe with an appropriately scaled Tongue Tie of scarlet lips and a protruding scarlet tongue.

Eight of the 17 exhibits in the Hasbro showrooms showed items new to the Hasbro line. Here's what Design Etc. did for three of these:

• For Cops 'n Crooks, which grew out of a comic book and TV cartoon series, they set up a fantasy jail. Cops 'n Crooks are 5½" solid plastic figures with arms that move. Each holds a tiny cap gun that fires a single cap. In a fantasy setting, Design Etc. made the walls and floors of chrome vinyl. The jail bars were curtain rods. Actors presenting the pitch stood

7.

9.

8.

behind the bars, often sharing the space with the Cops 'n Crooks figures, which were represented by cardboard cutouts 5' 4" high (just short of average human height). These fantasy figures had weapons, but, though violent, they were obviously cartoon figures, so the violence was cartoon violence. Design Etc. took color out of the space, then put color on the cardboard figures.

• Maxie is a new product created to compete with the legendary Barbie Doll. The Maxie line consists of Maxie Rob and three girlfriends, all seniors in high school and meant to fill a niche not filled by Barbie. Maxie's purchasers will be junior-high-school girls who look forward to being Maxie's age. Design Etc. put 9'-by-3' poster-like paintings of Maxie on the walls. These were drawn by illustrator Keith Batten in pastels on stretch canvas to emphasize her pretty face, her abundant blonde hair and her love of action. At the exhibit's entrance were a slew of Maxies and her friends set on 3' 9"-high, rose-colored block letters spelling out Maxie.

• B.A.B.Y. is a baby-like rag doll with a molded head that arrives on earth from outer space. None of the dolls are alike; in all, Hasbro estimates, there are 20,000 variations. They arrive on earth, the message goes, to learn something and one comes with its shoes untied, one with a brush and comb, and so on, and you, the purchaser, or the recipient, of a B.A.B.Y. become the teacher. To get across the idea of the arrival from outer space, Design Etc. set up a wooden, doll-like house

in front of a mural that showed light streaks heading from a distant planet toward a small town. These light streaks were fiber-optic rods with 4000 or 5000 light spots twinkling on them. The dolls were fastened to the mural near the light streaks and the illusion was that B.A.B.Y.s were comets raining down and bouncing from haystacks to rooftops. However, in a practical move, a group of the dolls were gathered on a roof-top blanket so that buyers could handle and inspect them.

Design Etc. designed and saw the exhibits fabricated and installed in five months, on a initial fabrication budget of $675,000. By watching materials' costs, they brought fabrication in for $624,000. The 1988 exhibit ran for eight months.

Client: Hasbro, Inc. (New York City)
Design firm: Design Etc., Inc., New York City
Designers: Don Campbell, Michael Maher, Tom Barnes, Fritz Conrad, Lizz Toma (visual merchandising), Trench Brady (assistant design and scenic artist), Andrea Jarnot (graphics), Anthony Kosiewska (purchasing and personnel coordination), Raphael Diaz (controller)
Consultants: Robert Strohmier (lighting), Ken Farley (special effects), Installation & Dismantle (installation, construction)
Fabricators: Art Guild (Maxie, My Little Pony); Constructive Displays (Maxie); Bruce & Bruce Stage Scenery (G.I. Joe, Cops 'n Crooks); Keith Batten (Maxie illustrations); Durawall, Stark Concepts, Systems Freestyle, Paris Lighting (Cops 'n Crooks); Innovations & the Friendly Lion (Maxie); Maxion Design (B.A.B.Y.); McHugh/Rollins Associates (Tongue Ties, B.A.B.Y.)

10.

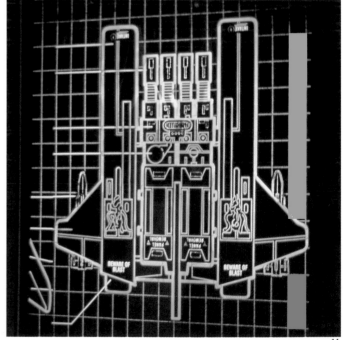

10. This is a space station built of tubes and Noracore triangular panels lighted from behind with neon. Airbrushed on the wall are planets and space clouds. The exhibit houses Hasbro toy line called Transformers (space-clad figures and their vehicles) and its packaging.
11. Detail from G.I. Joe exhibit, Hasbro's line of military dolls and vehicles. Neon outlines rocket ship against a grid.

11.

Clarks Originals

"Humor is so important," said one *Casebook* juror on first seeing slides of Clarks Originals trade show. Clarks of England has made shoes for more than 150 years. And Pentagram San Francisco designed this portable exhibit for them after designing a promotional campaign to help them "get serious" about selling their shoes in the U.S. Pentagram's promotional campaign for Clarks had included point-of-purchase displays, hang tags, packaging and a logotype, and for the trade show booth they blew up the logotype, mounted it on a foam-core laminate rising from slanted cylindrical base to 5′, and set one of these giant logo on each of three sides of the space (originally 20′ by 60′). The logotype has the two Clarks standing there in black-and-white looking like proper 19th-century merchants, one holding a Union Jack on a stick, lending the logo a splash of color. Circling their waists and dipping to their knees, like a life preserver or a broad hula hoop, is a cream-colored band that says Clarks Originals in black Bodoni Book letters.

Pentagram took that loop, sliced it in half and set it like an arch or a cream-colored rainbow — 4′ across — atop 18″-diameter, 8′-high Sonotube columns. Four arches and four Sonotubes (painted a deep blue, a shade deeper than the blue in the Union Jack, with red capitals, a shade brighter than the Union Jack red) form a square from the corners of which radiate 5′-high slat walls. Clear acrylic shelves in these slat walls hold Clarks shoes, lighted by fluorescent tubes in lightboxes atop the slat walls.

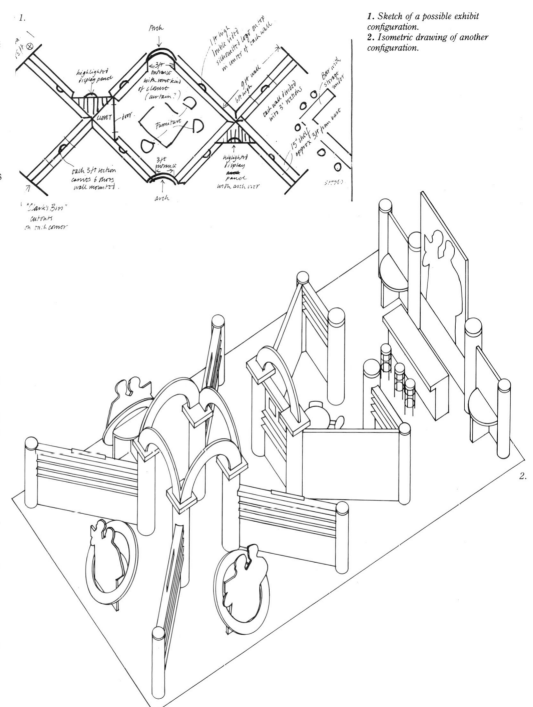

1. Sketch of a possible exhibit configuration.
2. Isometric drawing of another configuration.

Clarks wanted the exhibit to promote the national promotional campaign, too. Behind this cruciform grouping of shelves, columns and arches is a single arch. Between its supporting columns is a slat wall holding two framed copies of Clarks U.S. ads, and below the ads are examples of the available point-of-purchase displays that retailers could use. These are small cut-out figures of the Clarks (and their Union Jack) sticking up from Clarks shoes set on acrylic shelves. A small label on one of the Clarks'

left arm says something like "Our unique and revolutionary sole will have you walking on air." Or, "Air cushioning makes our accordion heel music to your feet." Neil Shakery, of Pentagram San Francisco, quickly notes, "We didn't compose these slogans."

Walls slanting toward the rear of the exhibit from this central arch enclose a conference area. And behind that, forming the exhibit's rear wall, is an 8'-high photo blowup of the Clarks. Seen from the front, they appear framed in a

series of arches. "Repetition," said one of the jurors, "is what caught the viewer's attention."

Clarks originally wanted a three- or four-stool bar in front of this end panel so that they could serve British ginger beer to visitors. But they couldn't find a supplier and the bar was taken out after the first installation, making no difference in the design. Indeed, the modular exhibit can be set up in almost any configuration.

Pentagram San Francisco designed and produced the

exhibit in three months on a total budget of $90,000.

Client: Clarks of England (Kennet Square, PA)
Design firm: Pentagram Design, Inc., San Francisco
Designers: Neil Shakery, Sandra McHenry
Consultant: John McConnell (Pentagram Design, London)
Fabricator: Exhibitgroup

3. The Clarks welcome visitors to their exhibit.
4. Racks of shoes radiate from central post-and-arch configuration.
5. Exhibit model.
6. Close-up of point-of-purchase display used in exhibit.

5.

4.

6.

Treasures of the Holy Land:
Ancient Art from the Israel Museum

The setting that Amy Forman of Amy Forman Design, Toronto, designed for this installation of "Treasures of the Holy Land" at Toronto's Royal Ontario Museum did two seemingly contradictory things. It allowed each of the show's 200 items to be seen individually without interference, and it gave visitors occasional glimpses of the breadth of the show, or at least large portions of it, imparting a sense of what they were seeing and where they were going. Just as important, Forman's design set a mood, creating through subtle plays of color and light a setting that evoked the earth and rocks of the Holy Land, a background against which these artifacts had originally been made and used.

Everything in the exhibit design went to give the artifacts—which ranged in size from a two-ton stone lion, 6' long and 3' high, to pieces of jewelry and animal head

carvings scarcely an inch or two across—a chance to be seen and savored in their best light, with no interference from the surroundings or other artifacts. For instance, one entered past a 6'-tall by 14'-long wall-mounted map of the Mediterranean (with an inset of the Holy Land) cut out of ½" plywood. This map was in what amounted to an entrance corridor whose walls angled in to frame one's focus on a cruciform arrangement of four 16"-by-16" vitrines, raised 3'8" on pedestals, that held the show's first five artifacts. Once past the map, the space opened to the full corridor width so that the vitrines seemed centered in a spacious setting, and beyond them, as a backdrop, Forman created a wall niche. Nothing stood in this niche; painted the same uniform medium gray as the walls of the entire exhibit ("She had the daring to use one color throughout," a *Casebook* juror said), the niche served as a sculptured backdrop for the

centrally-placed vitrines.

Forman used similar niches three times in the exhibition, positioning them to form a backdrop for vitrines holding small objects. Within the wall sections built out to form the niches, she placed wall cases. The first of these, just beyond the exhibit's first four vitrines, held an 8" clay head from Jericho dating from 7000 B.C. For risers and labels in case interiors, Forman specified a light gray and in the wall cases she covered the walls with a brown gray velour.

"The Treasures of the Holy Land," the largest, most important exhibition of ancient art to travel outside Israel, stopped in North America at the Metropolitan Museum of Art in New York, the Los Angeles County Museum of Art, and the Museum of Fine Arts, Houston, before reaching Toronto. The artifacts came from Israel arranged chronologically by age, starting with pre-history and moving through the Iron and

1.

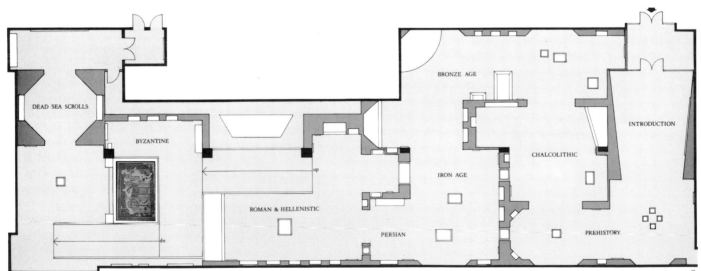

2.

1. Two-foot-high clay jar, of the type the Dead Sea Scrolls were found in, glows in exhibit light.
2. Floor plan.
3, 4. Ramp leads past Corinthian column and sarcophagus to a mosaic set into the floor. Beyond it, Dead Sea Scroll jar glowed through a scrim. Changing levels on ramp gave visitors different perspectives.

3.

4.

Bronze Ages to Roman and then Byzantine times, and each installation showed them in that sequence.

At the Royal Ontario Museum, Forman set up her exhibit along a serpentine path through the 8000-sq.-ft. exhibit hall. "It was like a maze," she says, "but I didn't want to convey the tension of being in a maze. I don't like it when I can't see where I'm going." To open up the spaces visually, she removed the backs of three wall recesses so that they became openings in the wall. Visitors could see through the recesses, past the pedestal-mounted vitrines in them, to the exhibit beyond. Two of these wall openings lined up. Looking through both of them, visitors had a view for 115', almost the entire length of the exhibit, to a 2'-high-1'-wide clay jar, the kind that held the Dead Sea Scrolls in the caves of Qumram. As one moved through the exhibit, one glimpsed this jar ahead, glowing ethereally through a scrim just in front of it, in the light of three low-voltage overhead spots. It pulled you toward it, without your knowing what it was, in what more than one visitor likened to a religious experience.

In setting up the exhibit, the large pieces went in place first. A fork-lift truck and a gantry crane moved these pieces into the space, artifacts like the two-ton stone lion, a 7'2"-high stone column 18½" in diameter with a Corinthian capital, the 200-pound piece of rock with Pontius Pilate's name carved into it (the only known archeological evidence of his existence, said by many to be

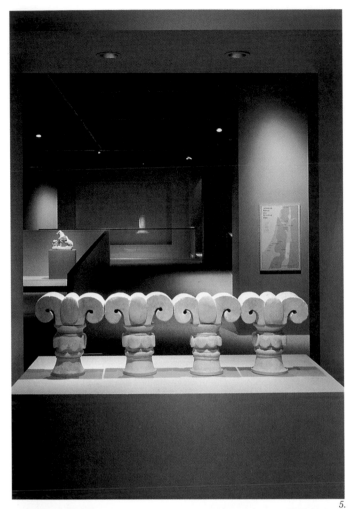

the show's most important piece) and the 10'-by-14' mosaic floor from a Byzantine synagogue.

Once these were settled, the exhibit was completed around them. Forman had the mosaic, which came in three steel-encased sections, set up on the floor, then built a platform 21" off the floor from which to view it. Situated on two sides of the mosaic, the viewing platform was screened from the mosaic by waist-high plexiglass topped by a wooden hand rail. Behind the mosaic was the 7'4" by 11'-8" scrim through which the Dead Sea Scroll jar glowed. To the left, a ramp led down to the jar and the shrine-like space Forman designed beyond it where she mounted two fragments of Dead Sea Scrolls in wall cases.

One approached the Byzantine mosaic on a 9'-wide, 27'-long ramp which rose to the mosaic past a wall-recessed platform on which stood the Corinthian column, a 6' limestone sarcophagus, and two Ossuaries (which once held bones).

In a niche across from the foot of this ramp, Forman recessed the 200-pound stone with the inscription referring to Pontius Pilate. By recessing it, she gave it some protection, but more than that, the recess provided a needed frame for the hunk of stone. "At first," she says, "the stone was not visually compelling." But this frame and a strong raking light from above lent it a sense of importance.

In laying out the exhibit, Forman left enough space at two points so that groups could gather, at the entrance by the wall map and on the platform overlooking the Byzantine mosaic. But, she says, "I didn't want to design exclusively for groups and overlook the mainstay of the museum: the individual visitor." For tired individuals, she tucked a couple of benches discreetly along walls in corners where people could rest and observe the exhibit without being on display themselves.

Forman Design had 10 months to design and produce the exhibit on a production budget of $150,000.

The *Casebook* jurors felt the simplicity and clarity of presentation focused attention on the exhibit's artifacts. Said one: "The exhibit was classic."

Client: Royal Ontario Museum (Toronto)
Sponsors: Dept. of Communications, Government of Canada; Dept. of Secretary of State of Canada; Canadian Friends of the Israel Museum, and other interested individuals, foundations, and businesses.
Design firm: Amy Forman Design, Toronto
Designer: Amy Forman
Consultants: Miriam Tadmor (curator, Israel Museum), Dan Rahimi (guest curator, Toronto), Paul Martinovich (ROM project coordinator), Eric Siegrist (ROM graphic designer), Gerry Mallette (ROM design technologist), Gerry Cornwell (lighting)
Fabricator: Shandon Associates Ltd.

5.

6.

7.

5. Corinthian balustrade set in open niche. Opening the niche allowed visitors to see through the entire exhibit to the glowing Dead Sea Scroll jar.
6. Viewers overlooking a Byzantine mosaic.
7. Some smaller, more delicate items were enclosed in vitrines.

Treasure Houses of Britain: 500 Years of Private Patronage and Art Collecting

For Gaillard F. Ravenel, chief of the Design and Installation Department at the National Gallery Art in Washington, DC, part of what made the Gallery's "Treasure Houses of Great Britain" a particular pleasure was the opportunity to help select the items that would ultimately be displayed in the exhibition. These items, furniture, paintings, sculpture, ceramics, armor, silver, and tapestries, all came from British country houses and all were displayed in settings that represented (but did not copy exactly) rooms in these beautiful country manors.

Actually, the exhibit had four designers. Besides Ravenel, there were Mark Leithauser and Gordon Anson, of the Gallery's Design and Installation Department, with whom he had worked for more than a decade. They had the enthusiastic help and guidance of Gervase Jackson-Stops, who is architectural advisor to the National Trust in London, which owns and administers some 100 of the grand English country houses and who served as curator for this show.

In a way, J. Carter Brown, the National Gallery's director, was a fifth member of the design team. The exhibition had been his idea. As a boy, he'd spent a year at a British boarding school housed in the country house of the Dukes of Buckingham, and he has stated that he began then "to sense that these houses were more than just playthings . . . that they were great intellectual centers . . . great centers of civilization." What Brown envisioned, and what "Treasure Houses of Britain" became, was

"an exhibition about the British country house as a work of art and creation of British genius, and as a kind of crystallization of a civilized approach to life over a long period of time."

"Treasure Houses" evolved into the most ambitious exhibition ever put on by the National Gallery, covering 35,000 sq. ft. of space, comprising 17 settings in 20 rooms on two levels of the museum's East Wing and consuming several years of

planning, selection, design, and construction. And though no one is talking officially about the budget, a spokesman for the Ford Motor Company, which sponsored the exhibit, has said that the cost ran well into seven figures and that Ford promised sufficient funds to assure that the exhibition took place.

Leithauser, Ravenel and Brown together made many trips to England, visiting as many as 200 English country homes either with or at the

suggestion of Gervase Jackson-Stops. Jackson-Stops also gathered, and arranged in categories, photocopies of art treasures displayed in these houses that might be loaned to the exhibit. There were not just great paintings, collected by owners of the houses, but also porcelain, silver, armor, sculpture, chairs, chests, couches, tapestries, sconces, jewels, vermeil, manuscripts, and drawings. It became apparent that any exhibition of

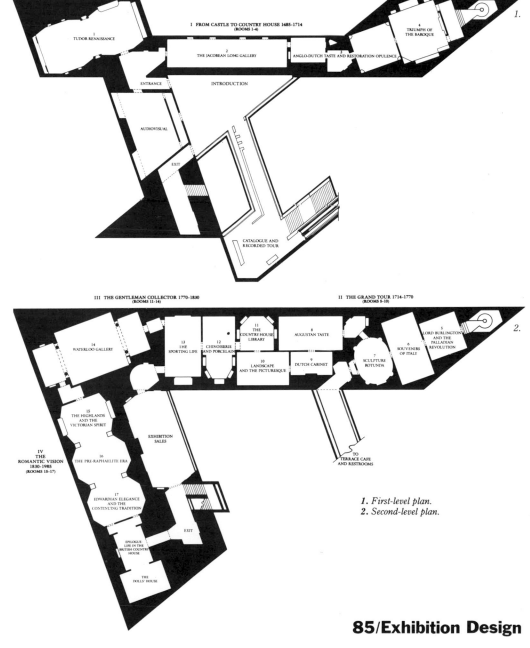

1. First-level plan.
2. Second-level plan.

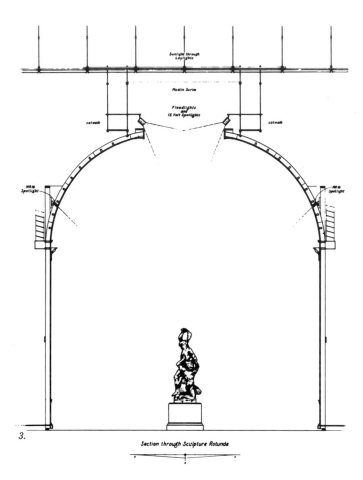

3.

Section through Sculpture Rotunda

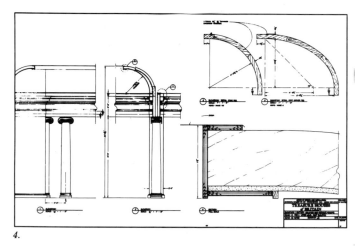

4.

these treasures would lose its meaning if they were just displayed in a conventional museum setting. What helped make them special was the context in which they were collected and lived with. Their architectural surroundings were part of the treasure. The columns, door frames, wall coverings, pilasters, moldings, ceiling beams, and window treatments were art, too, representative of the period in which the more movable items had been collected. The designers wanted to recreate these rooms as settings within the museum, but they realized that copying an existing room would defeat their purpose. If they recreated a particular room, they could display in it only the items that specifically belonged there. But they were collecting what they considered to be the best art from a host of houses. To do justice to all of these art objects, they decided to design room settings that included architectural details of the period in which the art had first been collected. This also allowed them to control the settings, creating just enough detail to tell their visual story without overpowering the pieces, creating a mood and a period as well as a setting with color, form and detail.

Borrowing details from old prints and paintings that showed rooms in country houses and from the houses themselves, they created 17 rooms, each typical of a certain period and of certain types of rooms found in the houses. These became the settings for the other art.

Mark Leithauser, who trained as an artist before becoming an exhibition designer, did careful drawings of these exhibit rooms and of the art pieces they might contain. The drawings became ways of determining what piece might go where, but more than that, they became a tool of persuasion that Gervase Jackson-Stops could use in trying to persuade owners to lend pieces to the exhibit.

More than architectural detail went into designing the rooms. Ravenal, Leithauser, and Gordon Anson, who does the lighting design and handles the production, spent time shaping the rooms, so that the configuration of each is an approximation of a similar room in a British country house. But in the National Gallery, the designers had more freedom and they carefully controlled room shape, ceiling height and lighting to create what Ravenel calls "grand spaces." For instance, you entered the sculpture rotunda room by first passing through two low-ceilinged rooms—one cube-shaped, one rectangular—and then into the rotunda with its oval floor plan beneath a 30′ domed ceiling. Though smaller than the two preceding rooms, the rotunda seems larger. Anson washed it with light from floodlights and then pinpointed the sculpture, the centrally placed *Samson and the Philistines* by Vincenzo Foggini, and other pieces in wall niches and roundels, with 12-volt spotlights hidden within the oculus at the top and with spots in the lower portion of the dome. The staff formed the dome by wetting drywall and shaping it over wooden supports and molded the niches of fiberglass. The rotunda was

meant to evoke the sculpture galleries that evolved in British country houses, like the one Robert Adam designed for Newby Hall in Yorkshire.

The exhibit's sequence told the story of the houses, their collections and the collectors chronologically. To do this, the designers divided the rooms into four overall historical sections:

1. From Castle to Country House 1485-1714.

2. The Grand Tour 1714-1770.

3. The Gentleman Collector 1770-1830.

4. The Romantic Vision 1830-1985.

In the Jacobean Long Gallery, the designers made the windows with leaded glass, whose green color, as well as the shapes of the windows and their detailing, were copied by Mark Leithauser from windows at Hardwick Hall. The ceiling was taken from a ceiling in Arundel Castle seen over the right shoulder of the Countess of Arundel in an early 17th-century portrait by Daniel Mytens that hangs in the exhibit's Long Gallery. That gallery's beamed ceiling hid lighting and held air-conditioning ducts. The designers glazed the walls, as they did most of the exhibit's walls, stippling and layering them to give a sense of age to the paint so that it would not clash with the pictures or their frames. Here, the color was a warm brown taken from the Mytens painting. And on top of the wall paint, artist Dieter Pluntke painted jagged cracks which looked original and old. They copied a door lintel from one at Castle Ashby in Northamptonshire and based

3, 4. Section and detail of exhibit's Sculpture Rotunda.
5. Sculpture Rotunda. Note arched and circular wall niches. Details in all the exhibit rooms came from detailing found in British country houses.
6. Ceiling in the exhibit's Jacobean Long Gallery was copied from one in Arundel Castle. Sisal mat on floor, 88' long, imitates those used in 18th century.

the window seats on ones Leithauser found at Kirby. On the room's 88' by 22' floor, a sisal mat imitated the rush matting used in the 18th century.

The designers paid this same meticulous attention to moldings (which they had cast from foam to plaster), wall papers (most hand-printed from antique blocks), baseboards and chair rails. Most of the furniture positioned along the walls was raised 4" or so on platforms made of chestnut flooring which had been in use in the National Gallery's West Wing for 45 years and had a sheen of use and care. Speaking of the National Gallery's exhibit designers, Gervase Jackson-Stops said: "I was unprepared for their astonishing attention to detail."

But, of course, detail is the glue that holds any well-designed exhibit together, and here designers Ravenel, Leithauser and Anson had a chance to indulge in plenty of it.

The exhibit's Waterloo Gallery, for instance, is loosely based on a picture gallery which John Nash designed in 1807 for Attingham Park in Shropshire. The Pompeian red on the walls was a copy of color used at Attingham. When Ravenel and Leithauser were there, they found that a console had been pulled away from the walls for repair and the original paint behind it still held its color. This is the color they copied. The Ionic columns in the Waterloo Gallery, also based on some found at Attingham, were made of wood with plaster capitals, then painted to look like porphyry.

In the exhibit's Dutch

7.

8.

9.

7. Exhibit's Dutch Cabinet section. Bronzes on the mantel and the painting above it are those seen in the painting to the right of doorway.
8. The Sporting Life gallery. Most of show's furniture was on 4" platforms along the walls.
9. Fireplace with porcelain collection.
10. Highlands and Victorian Spirit gallery with Corinthian columns.
11. Armor and weapons from the years 1485 to 1714, when country houses were replacing castles.

10.

11.

Cabinet, the designers took the wall color from the 1769 painting by Johan Zoffany, *Sir Lawrence Dundas and His Grandson*, in the Pillar Room at 19 Arlington Street. That picture hangs in the Dutch Cabinet and it shows Dundas sitting in front of a fireplace with the painting called *A Calm* done in 1654 by Jan van de Cappelle hanging over it. The designers found van de Cappelle's painting at another treasure house, Aske Hall, and hung it over a fireplace in the Dutch Cabinet. On the mantel were six small bronzes, the same ones seen in Zoffany's painting of Dundas and his grandson.

The National Gallery designers had labels screened on aluminum plaques for the platforms holding furniture and sculpture. They painted the aluminum to look like the wood it rested on and used large type so that visitors could read it without bending over. For labels of things hanging on the walls or placed in wall niches, they screened text directly on the walls to keep the labels from being obtrusive. For their typeface, they chose Galliard because it is English with a classic Roman look, and it was close to the typeface used in the catalogue.

The exhibit was spare and well-paced. The designers eliminated the need for a lot of text by starting the exhibit with an audiovisual show which explained it, then handing everyone who entered a brochure with a room-by-room guide.

The rooms were uncluttered, the art given space to breathe and be seen, and the overall effect was one of calm, serenity and peace, or would have been without the 700 visitors an hour that the National Gallery filtered through the show. They came without let-up, hour after hour, for the entire three-and-a-half months the exhibit was in place, until almost a million persons had seen it.

At the entrance, on the National Gallery's East Wing mezzanine, a felt banner with the exhibit's title stretched along two sides of the mezzanine beneath a Calder mobile that hangs there. On one wall beneath the banner was an 88'-long photo blowup of an engraving of Blenheim Palace in Oxfordshire, which the designers mounted on the wall like wallpaper. On the other wall, visitors could enter the explanatory audiovisual show through a blowup of the entrance to Syon House in Middlesex. Or they could enter the exhibit directly through a door just to the right of the audiovisual show entrance.

All gold and silver objects in the exhibit were displayed behind plexiglass, in cases that had a newly installed, sophisticated security system. The designers didn't want anything behind the ropes, believing that would detract from the country-house atmosphere, so the Gallery beefed up its usual staff of security guards.

If "Treasure Houses of Britian" leaves a legacy, it is reinforcement of the certainty that fine art can be enhanced by the settings in which it is displayed.

As Gervase Jackson-Stops put it: " . . . exhibitions that deal with art collecting on a broad scale, or attempt to

explain the function of taste at a certain period, need to do more. They need to set works of art in a context where the whole is more important than the sum of the parts; where disparate objects speak to each other in a setting that both enhances their appearance and makes them more comprehensible."

Client: National Gallery of Art (Washington, DC)
Sponsor: Ford Motor Co.
Design firm: Design and Installation Dept., National Gallery of Art
Designers: Gaillard F. Ravenel (chief), Mark Leithauser (deputy chief); Gordon Anson (lighting design, head of production); Barbara Keyes, Fred Parker (graphic design); Floyd Everly (head of exhibit construction)
Consultants: Gervase Jackson-Stops (curator), Chris Vogel (typesetting), Richard Humphries (fabric weaving), Dieter Pluntke (specialty painting)
Fabricator: Exhibits Shop, National Gallery of Art

12. Chinoiserie and Porcelain gallery. Bed canopy, never before used, had been stored in attic of British country house for 200 years.

12.

An American Sampler: Folk Art from the Shelburne Museum

Chance led to the National Gallery of Art's exhibition of 120 works of art from the Shelburne Museum in northern Vermont. The National Gallery's deputy director, John Wilmerding, is vice-president of Shelburne's board of trustees. His grandmother, Electra Havemeyer Webb, founded the Shelburne Museum to display the furniture and early American art she had collected for 35 years. Noting that 1987 was the 40th anniversary of the Shelburne's founding, Wilmerding suggested the exhibit to honor the occasion.

It was fortuitous, too, that the National Gallery's exhibition designers, Gaillard F. Ravenel, Mark Leithauser and Gordon Anson, had only a year before created a setting for art from Great Britain's magnificent country houses (see "Treasure Houses of Britain" elsewhere in this book). From that exhibit, they had learned that art objects often enhance one another when seen together against a background similiar to that in which they were originally meant to be viewed.

So for the 120 quilts, wooden sculptures, whirligigs, wind vanes, decoys, hooked rugs, cigar-store Indians, gaily-painted carousel animals, store signs and furniture from the Shelburne's collection, they designed a four-room setting with details taken from the architecture of Shelburne's early New England buildings. The four rooms and two small connecting spaces on the upper level of the National Gallery's East Building gave the art 10,000 sq. ft of space, and evoked, through detailing, color, shape and proportions, the architectural feeling of old New England's houses, barns and store fronts. Colors on the walls, moldings and door frames came from those on 19th-century painted boxes. Pedestals on which many of the items were mounted (without vitrines) were made of fir and plywood (with detailing from an old Vermont house at Shelburne) and painted to look old by specialty painter Dieter Pluntke.

Also following their design direction for "Treasure

2.

Houses," the designers varied the size and shape of their rooms. Here, the spaces flowed together with only two articulated transitions. Between the first and second rooms was a corridor with a central pedestal-mounted swift (used for winding yarn) standing beneath hanging signs: an optician shop's 7'-long gilded spectacles, a locksmith's 3' key, a dentist's 2' molar sign, and an 8' carved wooden rifle which once announced a gunsmith. Between the third and fourth rooms, to mark a

transition from a room running north and south to one running east and west, was a small connecting space designed like a roundhouse. It contained a single railroad-engine weathervane of sheet zinc and iron bars. Dieter Pluntke painted the room's wood-slatted walls blue with a buttermilk-based paint he mixed himself. Overhead was a skylight of wooden ribs and scrim.

The final artifacts room, filled with quilts and weather vanes, was octagonal, like an octagonal New England barn. To heighten the atmosphere, Gordon Anson's lighting threw weathervane shadows on the walls between quilts.

Quilts hung on the walls of every room, giving the exhibit continuity and wonderful splashes of pattern, texture and color. One room had a group of boldly-painted carousel animals on an octagonal oak platform. Over the platform hung a pinwheel with wooden spokes painted the same powder-blue of the walls. "We tried to saturate the space," says Ravenel, and this they did without ever sacrificing a sense of order and calm. They managed to give everything its own isolation, while making sure that nearby objects complemented one another and that sight lines led you to see one thing against another, such as wooden sculpture or carousel animals against quilts. "It became a three-dimensional collage," says Ravenel.

But because of the charm and color of the objects and the way the designers arranged them, the exhibit also had a sense of fun, of playfulness and innocence. As you entered the

1.

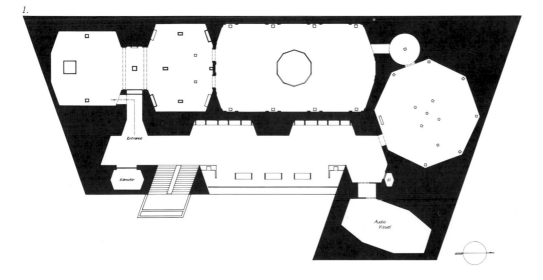

1. Floor plan.
2. Wall-hung quilts form backdrops for furniture and carvings.

first of the four rooms, you passed a 5'-long, gaily painted carp with a flag rising from its back. It had been over a bar somewhere in New York State before moving to the Shelburne, and the designers mounted it with an armature on a single piece of plexiglass, set like a window into a wall. You could see past the carp to the interior of the exhibit. From inside, the carp was still visible, and set the tone for the show.

Here, as in the "Treasure Houses" exhibit, the designers had a hand in selecting what would be displayed. In fact, they made the initial selection for "American Sampler." On a trip to Vermont, Ravenel and Leithauser picked 160 items from the Shelburne's collections to exhibit in Washington. The curators reduced this number to 110, and on a second trip to Vermont the designers added another 12, from which the curators subtracted one, to end up with 121. So almost everything shown was selected with more than one eye on how it would enhance the exhibit visually. Much of the exhibit's lighthearted feeling and sense of fun probably stems from this kind of selection.

Ravenel and Leithauser felt strongly that to put these objects in vitrines would be to work against their appeal. Not only would they lose something from reflections in the plexiglass, but they would also be isolated from the surroundings in which they are meant to be seen. So only small scrimshaw pieces (such as pie crimpers) and decoys and fragile bird carvings were placed in wall cases and even these were designed to look,

3.

4.

5.

not like cases, but like store fronts or shop windows with glass on three sides, and lights in lift-up bonnets.

For security, the designers "saturated the space with guards" and in front of each quilt they placed a rope strung between calf-high posts to keep visitors at least 3' away.

Light shown only on the objects, because any more than seven-foot candles of illumination in the space would have damaged the quilts. This lighting helped create an illusion that some of the items were floating in space, a sense that deepened the feeling of calm and fun. "We meant it as a celebration of delight," says Ravenel, "a celebration of the spirit Mrs. Webb had in putting her collections together."

Labels in Clearface type were screened directly on walls, platforms and pedestals. On the carousel platform, the labels went on bevelled pieces of wood, stained and pickled to look like the oak of the platform.

Before entering the exhibit, you passed a 10' flat carving of one of the show's weathervanes (a kneeling Indian aiming an arrow toward the exhibit's entrance), wall-mounted beneath the show's title in Cochin typeface.

At the end, you could go into a fifth room, a 2500-sq.-ft. theater, and see an audiovisual show about Mrs. Webb and Shelburne and its architecture. "We wanted people to see the objects first, then be able to put them in context," explains Ravenel, "and then we hoped, once they'd seen the slide show, they'd go back through the exhibit."

6.

7.

Client: National Gallery of Art (Washington, DC)
Sponsor: The New England (Boston)
Design firm: Design and Installation, National Gallery of Art
Designers: Gaillard F. Ravenel, Mark Leithauser, Gordon Anson (lighting and head of production), Barbara Keyes (graphics), Floyd Everly (head of exhibit construction), Chris Vogel (typesetting)
Consultants: John Wilmerding (deputy director, National Gallery of Art); Linda Ayers (curator); Robert Shaw (curator, Shelburne Museum); curators at National Gallery and at Shelburne; Dieter Pluntke (specialty painting)
Fabricator: Exhibits Shop, National Gallery of Art

3. Carp with flag rising from its back is mounted on single plexiglass sheet to let visitors see past it to the exhibit beyond.
4. Carousel animals displayed on octagonal oak platform with quilts behind them.
5. Locomotive weathervane in round, skylighted room forms transition between two larger exhibit rooms.
6. Gilded spectacles, once an optician's sign, and 2' molar (a dentist's sign) hang at exhibit entrance. Designers placed only small, fragile objects in vitrines or wall cases and designed wall cases to look like shop windows.
7. Wooden carving against quilt and wall case.

A Century of Modern Sculpture:
The Patsy and Raymond Nasher Collection

For six months in late 1987 and early 1988, sculptures from Patsy and Raymond Nasher's remarkable collection of 20th-century (and some late 19th-century) sculpture were shown in Washington, DC's National Gallery of Art. That the 68 sculptures looked almost as comfortable there in the Gallery's open spaces as they had in the Nashers' Dallas garden was a credit to the Gallery's Design and Installation Department, and to those who helped them.

It started with a visit made by National Gallery director J. Carter Brown to the Nashers' home. Highly impressed with their magnificent sculpture collection of more than 100 pieces, situated in their Lawrence Halprin-designed garden as well as within their house, Brown conceived an exhibition at the National Gallery that would use the Gallery's open spaces, turning them into a garden for the sculpture. These spaces offered some 20,000 sq. ft.—on the concourse, ground floor and mezzanine of the Gallery's I.M. Pei-designed East Wing, outside on the building grounds, in part of the West Building and on top of an outside sculpture pool, which was turned into a sculpture terrace. The space worked out to almost 300 sq. ft. for each of the 68 sculptures, enough room for them to express their individuality. It was the designers' task to see that they weren't overshadowed by the building and that they didn't clash with it. The garden spaces designed by Gaillard F. Ravenel and Mark Leithauser and the lighting by Gordon Anson went

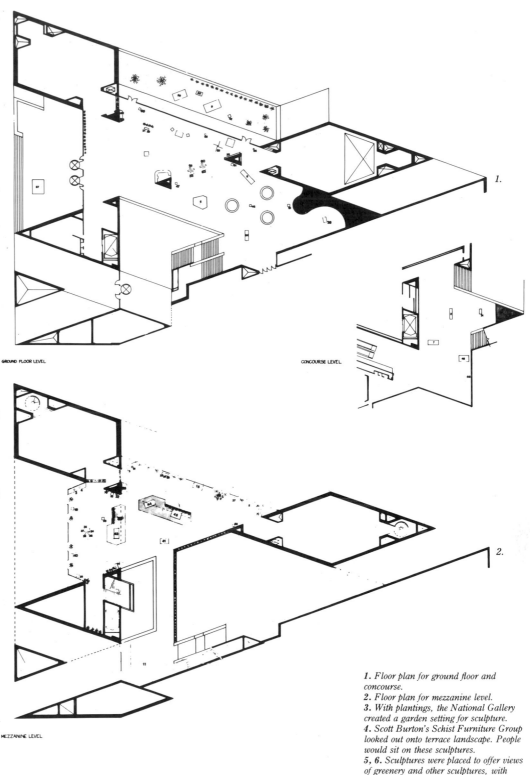

GROUND FLOOR LEVEL

CONCOURSE LEVEL

1.

2.

MEZZANINE LEVEL

1. Floor plan for ground floor and concourse.
2. Floor plan for mezzanine level.
3. With plantings, the National Gallery created a garden setting for sculpture.
4. Scott Burton's Schist Furniture Group looked out onto terrace landscape. People would sit on these sculptures.
5, 6. Sculptures were placed to offer views of greenery and other sculptures, with sufficient room to give each piece its own space.

3.

4.

5.

6.

a long way toward assuring harmony. The remaining relationship between building and sculpture grew from placing each piece in a spot that suited it.

From two earlier sculpture shows — one of David Smith's works, the other of Rodin's — Ravenel and Leithauser knew something of what kind of sculpture worked well in which spaces. They knew, for instance, that human-sized figures had been shown to advantage on the mezzanine and that Smith's work had looked especially good on the ground floor of the East Wing. The show's largest work, Jonathan Borofsky's 20'-high Hammering Man, was so heavy that it could only go on a piling on the concourse level.

Working with a large floor plan on paper, the designers moved small cutouts of each sculpture around until they found a suitable space. Then they helped the placement along by covering some of the East Building's glossy marble wall surfaces with dryboard coated with a mixture of tiny pieces of quartz crystals in epoxy resin that produces a rough, stone-like surface. They gave it a warm beige color, and they used it on more than the walls. It covered, for instance, the partitions built under the mezzanine overhang to break the transition from a low ceiling space to the 70'-height of the atrium. Those partitions sheltered smaller pieces and offered surprises as you discovered new sculptures in each partioned area. In all the placements, the designers tried to match the scale of the sculpture to the scale of the

building. By arranging each piece so it could be encountered from many angles, they enabled visitors to experience it fully. Pedestals covered in the same beige rough coating raised some of the sculptures to eye level, setting them off, says Ravenel, "the way a frame does a picture." The plantings were part of the setting, too, of course. And for these Ravenel and Leithauser designed large plywood planting boxes, covered in the same sand and epoxy coating and lined with roofing material. Donald Hand, the museum horticulturist, filled these planters with hedges and other plants and they became the interior garden that Carter Brown had originally envisioned.

The designers covered the East Building's large expanses of glass with baffles, cutting the outside light so that there was enough to silhouette the sculpture but not enough to create vision-obscuring glare.

One of the *Casebook* jurors said of the installation: "It was an excellent solution of space utilization in one of the most difficult exhibition areas in the country."

In some spaces, you could see the sculpture outside through the glass. Just outside the entrance stood George Segal's grouping of bronze-clad commuters which he calls "Rush Hour," and on the Gallery grounds were other large works by Tony Smith, Alain Kirili, Joan Miro, and others.

Patsy and Raymond Nasher took great interest in the exhibition's design, flying to Washington to check its progress and offering helpful

suggestions. "They understand the objects well," Ravenel says. And he remembers, at one point, Carter Brown and Raymond Nasher deciding to continue an interior hedge row on the concourse out onto the sculpture terrace so that the glass wall between them would not be so intrusive. The two chairs and a settee of Scott Burton's Schist Furniture Group looked out onto the terrace through that glass wall and occasionally during the exhibit people would come and sit on them and gaze at the pieces on the terrace.

The arrangement of the sculptures wasn't random, even if it seemed so. They were grouped historically and by artist, with one grouping of, say, Moore's offering sight lines to an arrangement of Giacometti's, and so on. Small pieces and fragile ones like Rodin's plaster "Head of Balzac" went in vitrines, and everything was fastened down, anchored to the pedestals by armatures. Each pedestal had a door in its side so that the staff could reach in and fasten the armature. Once that was done, they spackled the opening before covering it with the pedestal's rough beige coating.

Sometimes the design department screened labels right on the floor in large Omega typeface. For the smaller pieces on pedestals, the labeling type went directly on the pedestals.

Lighting came mostly from overhead spots, some as far as 70′ above the sculptures, and was a careful arrangement of low- and high-voltage.

The designers had a year to design and install the exhibit on a budget, not disclosed, that was donated by Northern Telecom.

Client: National Gallery of Art (Washington, DC)
Sponsor: Northern Telecom
Design firm: Design and Installation Dept., National Gallery of Art
Designers: Gaillard F. Ravenel, Mark Leithauser, Gordon Anson (lighting, production head), Barbara Keyes (graphics), Floyd Everly (head, exhibit construction), Gloria Randolph, Chris Vogel (typesetting)
Consultants: Steven Nash (curator, Dallas Museum of Art), Nan Rosenthal (curator, National Gallery of Art)
Fabricator: Exhibits Shop, National Gallery of Art

7. *Dubuffet sculpture against trees at exhibit entrance.*
8. *Some sculpture was set right in the greenery.*
9. *Some smaller, more fragile pieces like this Rodin plaster head were placed in vitrines.*